JOHN ALEXANDER

Shadows

of

Secret Lives

For Lori, whose belief in me never wavered.

This book is as much yours as it is mine.

Acknowledgments

Many thanks to my wife, Lori, my two sisters, Frances and Estelle, and my friend, Jill Caldwell, who read the early drafts of this story and gave me feedback on the inconsistencies and errors.

I sincerely appreciate your encouragement to continue writing.

Preface

Set in 1974 in Maine and Cornwall, England, the story is about the conflict and eventual resolution arising from discovering secrets that profoundly affect the characters.

Long shadows are cast over Caroline Hall, the daughter of Henry Stern, the head of an international trucking and shipping company, who goes missing. As she uncovers hidden secrets, she and her husband, Robert, piece together the details of her father's history. As the years of concealment are unveiled, hope and the possibility of forgiveness and understanding emerge.

There are things about our parents we do not know.
Knowing their secrets could do more harm than good.
Some secrets should be allowed to die with them.

Prologue

Coast of Cornwall, England 1944

Eight-year-old children should be home in bed sleeping, not walking around a hillside on the coast of England in the dark. This child was wearing a heavy wool coat, the cuffs a little worn, and mud stains around the bottom from an outing searching for wild mushrooms with Mum. Underneath the coat are the favorite pajamas, light blue with clouds blending to dark blue with stars and the moon. Made from rich cotton, they were warm and cozy, a gift from a loving parent at a time when most anything of comfort was hard to come by.

The German forces were patrolling the body of water between France and England. To the English, it is 'The Channel. 'The French call it 'La Manche' (The Sleeve). Nazi Germany was trying to regain control of the war in Europe. Everyone hoped and prayed it would soon end. Only then could security and peace be found in their lives, to raise children, see them grow, and have children of their own.

It is hard to imagine how war seems through the eyes of a child. It is unimaginable. For children, there can be no real explanation.

Nothing a parent can say makes sense beyond "We

are good, and they are bad." In times of war, children need to know there are dangers, so we scare them with stories that will keep them safe.

The child looked down 50 feet to the cove below; shadows were moving here and there. Over the sound of waves crashing onto the stony beach, someone could be heard shouting. Then, BANG, a gunshot, a woman screamed, and a shadow fell— another BANG, another gunshot, soon followed by more shouting. Then BANG, BANG, two more shots sounding like the circus lion tamer's whip.

Trying to understand what is happening, the child's imagination goes to extreme places as fear sears the heart. Without thinking, the child runs to escape and hide as adrenalin kicks in. Bedroom slippers fall from small feet and then a tumble, a fall. The child's head hits a rock; blood seeps slowly from head wounds, and all is dark.

Disappearance: Portland, Maine, 1974

"Line two, Caroline, it's the police."

Sitting at a desk in the corner office, Caroline Hall looked across the container terminal in Portland, Maine. She could see ships at the dock through the window to one side. The terminal could hold a thousand containers. With its Deepwater port, it could accommodate the biggest ships. It was the largest tonnage seaport in New England.

Caroline's mind was elsewhere as she studied the cranes pointing like accusatory fingers at the sky and beyond them, the Casco Bay Bridge, now partially concealed in the damp mist. Shipping containers were hanging from cranes as they moved slowly back and forth. The operator was carefully loading them onto ships for export and trucks that would take the imported merchandise from around the world to other inland destinations along the Eastern Seaboard and beyond.

An eighteen-wheeler was backing up, and off to one side, watching its progress, a man was holding a walkie-talkie to his mouth, a yellow hard hat on his head. Dressed in yellow waterproof pants over large boots and an orange coat with ST&S in six-inch black letters across the shoulders, he raised his free hand, and the truck stopped, and he walked toward the driver 'scab.

The heavy rain that had started earlier that morning had begun to ease, and the last few days had seen a winter warm-up, a welcome break to the implacable cold and snow, usual for Maine during winter.

Caroline's attention was drawn to a red brick building across the yard. It was a converted receiving shed and now the architectural offices of her husband, Robert Hall. Water was running from a broken gutter; she grits her teeth and mutters, "damn thing should have been fixed weeks ago."

A couple of folders are on the desk in front of her, and behind her, in the middle of the room, is a conference table. On two walls, there are bookshelves with a collection of popular management know-how books—for example, Open to Change and Top Team Planning. There were also reference books, maps, encyclopedias, and a large dictionary. On the walls were pictures of other terminals in Canada and photos of her dad shaking hands with some people in front of a truck, the side of which proclaimed, "**Stern Trucking & Shipping.**"

This was the office of Henry Stern, Caroline's dad, the company founder. Over 25 years, Stern Trucking and Shipping have become highly regarded in the industry. It was a private company that Caroline had been involved with since graduating college. She understood how the business operated and knew some, but not all, of its secrets. Henry had always assumed, and Caroline had accepted, that one day she would take over the reins from her dad. But not like this. It's only been a few months since she started to ease back to work. Having raised her children, she thought it was time for her to start work again, but really, she was not ready, and certainly not ready to face the problems about to unfold.

Henry Stern was the driving force behind what had become the most prominent regional freight transport organization on the East Coast and was missing. He had just disappeared ten days ago, and no one had heard from him.

Based in Portland, Maine, Stern Trucking and Shipping had access to international terminals at docks, airports, and the highways that link the North American continent from coast to coast and in Canada, St. John, New Brunswick, and Quebec.

Caroline was telling herself the broken drainpipe was the least of her problems when her thoughts were interrupted by a voice on the intercom announcing Sergeant Hope. It brought her back into the room.

She ran her fingers through her red curly hair, which she occasionally tinted, trying to hide the effects of time and life's never-ending challenges. She wore it short and cut into the nape of her neck. Lines were beginning to appear on her face. They presented a challenge and a warning that her age was creeping up on her. But she liked who she was. Other people liked her, too. Her husband, Robert, often told her she had a powerful presence. Of course, she did not believe him, but if it were true, she probably inherited it from her dad. She lifted the phone from its cradle, stretched upright, and took a deep breath. Hoping for good news, she pushed the keypad's flashing button.

"It's Sergeant Hope, Mrs. Hall. Just returning your call." Police Sergeant Hope was now, sad to say, a familiar voice. Sergeant Hope said, "Since we last talked, we have looked through all airline and car rental company records and can find nothing...' Caroline interrupted.

"He may have used the jet. Did you check the airfield?"

Sgt. Hope added, ignoring the impatient tone, "We spoke to the pilot; the jet was grounded for the week before your dad disappeared. The plane is getting a C check."

Caroline interjected, "Oh, right, and the upgrades."

Sgt. Hope continued. "Normally, this would only take about a week to do, but he also scheduled an installation of new seats and a stereo system." "Right," Caroline said as she waited patiently for anything positive. Sergeant Hope continued, "Well, it's still waiting for parts and cannot fly. There are no further records of him using the plane. The airport maintenance people hadn't heard from him since the week before the plane was grounded when he returned from Canada. He has not used his credit cards, and the last time was for gas in Portland two days before he disappeared."

With the phone in her hand, Caroline turned from the desk and walked across the room to the conference table with a map, notepad, a few sheets of paper, an empty coffee cup, and an ashtray somebody should have emptied two hours ago. Picking up a pack of cigarettes, she shook one out, put it in her mouth, lit it, and blew the first puff of smoke off to one side. She had tried to quit many times and had tried everything, including meditation, yoga, and hypnotism, and nothing worked permanently.

She was on edge and openly smoking again. The uncertainty about decisions she needed to take, the exhausting confusion and anxiety of searching for answers to questions about where her dad could be, and the helplessness of not knowing got the better of her. She was short-tempered and irritable.

Caroline took a deep drag on the cigarette, inhaling the smoke into her lungs. Weary of excuses, standing at the end of the table with one eye on the broken, dripping gutter on the building across the yard, she said to Sgt Hope. "So far, you have come up with nothing, zero! How could a grown man disappear? One day here and the next gone. Nothing. No letter, phone call, airline reservation, or hotel reservation."

Sgt. Hope interrupted her. "Well, he did have a reservation in Boston for two nights at the Copley Plaza, but he didn't show up and did not cancel."

"Well, that's something. But why would my dad make a reservation and not show up? He must have been in an accident." Sergeant Hope said, "That's possible. There were a few accidents on the highway in the last few days, but nothing major, and certainly nothing that involved your father. And, Mrs. Hall, I know you want to keep things out of the press, but don't you think it's time to run a story in the local newspapers? Maybe some paid ads asking for help and a reward?"

I am not ready to take that step yet. I want to leave it for now. "I will think about it and let you know in a day or two." Sergeant Hope tried again. "You never know, and it is worth a try. Let the world know he is missing; maybe somebody will have seen him."

"No, not yet, Sergeant," she snarled, thinking how ironic his name is Hope, and he offers none.

Caroline, now angrier, "I told you that, for now, I must keep this out of the press. As far as I knew, he was attending a meeting in Boston. "She ground the half-burned cigarette into the ashtray, visualizing Sergeant Hope's face. "Maybe you should check again with the hospitals in Boston? Maybe he did go; something could have happened, and now he is in a hospital somewhere."

Sgt. Hope replied. "Yes, and he would have had some ID on him, and all accidents, especially those that involve hospitals, are reported. But in any case, we checked the hospitals along his possible route in New Hampshire and other parts of Massachusetts, but nothing came up. He was driving his dark green Jeep, right?"

Ever so slightly, narrowing her eyes and pursing her lips, "Yes." Caroline replied. "We also checked the tow companies in case his car was abandoned."

Caroline asked, "Why would he abandon his car? It's been freezing cold out there!"

Sgt Hope was trying to be conciliatory. "Well, that's true, but we have to check everything, just in case."

"Sergeant, I don't know what else to tell you, but please find my dad. Find out what has happened. Perhaps you should take a closer look at his house. Maybe something was missed last time?"

"We did. We looked. There was nothing out of order. It appeared your dad just left the house. There are no signs of a struggle; as I said, nothing out of order.

"Well, excuse me for saying so, but your look seemed fairly cursory and…"

Sgt. Hope interrupted again. "Yes, I can see how it would have appeared that way, but nothing indicated anything out of the ordinary, and we do not know what we are looking for. There was nothing to suggest a break-in, and nothing was disturbed."

* * *

Sergeant Hope flipped a switch on the recorder to block his voice and looked at the other officers listening. He opened his hands and lifted his head slightly to one side as if asking a question. Both the men, with a slight shrug and negatively shaking their heads, indicated 'no.'

When Caroline first spoke with Sergeant Hope, her husband, Robert, and her three children had been away, staying in their lodge at the Sugarloaf Mountain Ski Resort. They returned home to find a note from Caroline that her dad was missing, and she was at his house with the police. Robert arrived with the children after the police had left. "Where is Pops anyway," asked Michael, the oldest of their children, in that semi-interested, detached tone that teenagers seem to master.

She could only tell him, "I do not know." She hated it, hated not being in control. Henry had disappeared, vanished, and Robert wasn't any help. Now, the banks were pressuring her to make decisions, and Stern Trucking and Shipping's main competitor was putting pressure on her to continue with the negotiation to merge rather than go public or sell. Of course, none of this could happen. Life was on hold since Henry went missing.

* * *

"Sergeant, 1 have to meet with my board in twenty minutes. If you have nothing new for me, then I really must go. I appreciate your call and update, and I will call you if anything else comes up. Thank you for returning my call."

"I will call as soon as we find out anything."

"Thank you, sergeant, goodbye."

They both hung up the phone. Caroline went to the coffee machine in the corner of the office and ran a fresh brew, ready for the meeting with the board. Anxious about her ability to withstand the pressure any longer, she desperately tried to control things.

Half slumped over the coffee machine, shoulders bent forward as the gut feeling nagged at her, and her head telling her that any hope about him reappearing was fading. The days dragged on, and there was less chance to find him the longer he was missing. While she wanted to do everything possible to find him, Caroline needed to protect the business her dad had worked so hard on over many years. It was his life's work. Caroline had decided to keep his disappearance private to protect it as best she could. But she was conflicted and uncertain if it was the right thing to do. Aloud, and as if talking to the coffee machine, she asked, "What would Dad do?"

In times of stress, small, familiar things bring consolation. Small acts of routine, simple things help us calm our anxieties. She could have had Jenny McCarthy, Henry's secretary, get the coffee—this was his office, after all. But the machine was there, and making coffee gave her a sense of normalcy.

Still standing in front of the machine, watching the hot coffee drip into the glass flask, tears welled up. Sobbing almost silently, she took another deep breath, stretched, and straightened her shoulders. Talking to the coffee machine again, she mumbled quietly, "I can do this; keep it together; we will find out soon; it will be OK."

* * *

Back at the Portland police headquarters, Sergeant Hope put the phone down and turned to the other officer in the room. "Maybe we should go and take another look?"

Turning the tape recorder off, the officer pressed his lips together and shook his head from side to side, raising his eyebrows as if to say, 'Maybe.' "We did. It was a waste of time. Nothing was disturbed, and the place was well-kept. The bed was made, no dishes in the sink, the desk tidy, and anyway, what would we be looking for?"

"Yeah, you're probably right," Sergeant Hope replied. And there was nothing new in that phone call. Now, getting up and organizing the recorder and his notes, the officer said, "So, who stands to benefit if he never shows up?"

Sergeant Hope nodded in agreement, "She certainly does, and so does her husband, but it's not like they need money or anything. I think most likely he's in hiding, and maybe she knows it and is an excellent liar and a brilliant actor!"

"No, I don't think so," The officer replied. "I think she wants to find him as much as we do."

"Maybe, but in the meantime," Sergeant Hope said, lifting his right hand and clicking his fingers, "Poof! He is gone, and we don't know if he is dead, a prisoner, or hiding. We will have to keep looking." Then, glancing at his watch, "Shit, I must get going." He put on his coat and hat and, over his shoulder as he left the room,

"Let's talk later."

* * *

Caroline poured herself a fresh coffee and took it to the window next to the desk, opening it to let the chill air rush in and replace the smokey smell of her cigarettes. The rain had stopped, and clouds shifted as the sun tried to break through. She welcomed the cool breeze on her cheeks. Standing there for a minute, looking across the Terminal, she said aloud, "Dad, please come home." She took a few deep breaths and returned to the table.

Sitting at the head of the table, she ran the fingers of both hands through her hair, pushing it back, her fingers locked and cradling the back of her head. Her lips started to curl as she was again fighting her tears. Leaning forward, she closed her arms around her stomach, trying to push a queasy feeling away. She sat there in silence, gently rocking back and forth. Darkness swirled in her mind, and then, opening her eyes and picking up a pen, she reviewed a scribbled note she had made earlier:

Banks
Competitors
Board
Members
Press
Police
Kids
Robert. Underlining his name, she added to the list,
Where can Dad possibly be?

A Small One Can't Hurt

Robert Hall's office and design studio on the upper floor of the red brick building that was once a receiving shed now had exposed beams, heating ducts, and conduits that carried power lines across the ceiling. The exposed brick walls running both sides of the entire length of the room hung with drawings of past projects and conceptualizations of future projects that Robert hoped to work on one day. He was happy to be in his office, as much as anywhere. It was close to town and had interesting views of the working waterfront. But maybe it was a little too close to his wife since Henry disappeared.

He was dressed in jeans and a turtle-neck sweater and stood at his drafting table. The studio was big enough for him, an assistant, and one or two additional architects, even though working alone suited him.

Across from him on a workbench was a half-built model of a new Stern Trucking and Shipping building. Robert turned to the desk behind him. It was a thick glass top with beveled edges supported by trestles. Under the table to the right and in front of a comfortable desk chair was a free-standing set of draws on little caster wheels.

Robert sat down, opened the drawer, and took out a

bottle of vodka. It was empty with a note written in red ink and attached by sticky tape. "Robert, if you don't stop this, our marriage is over. if you have to go into rehab again, our marriage will be over."He ripped the note from the bottle, crumpled it into a tight ball, and threw it into a trash can behind his right shoulder. He put his elbows on the desk and, resting his forehead on his hands, sat there immobilized, his body craving the surge and then the relaxation of the alcohol.

Thirty seconds later, he got up and walked to the other end of the studio to the closet where he hung his coat this morning and changed from the sturdy winter boots to more comfortable casual boat shoes. Opening the closet, he took out a new bottle of vodka and a glass. Mumbling to himself, "She shouldn't be snooping around in my desk. Fucking nosy, that's what she is." Taking a shot from the bottle, he poured more into the glass, added tonic water and ice from the nearby refrigerator, and returned to his desk. Now feeling more relaxed, he studied the drawing of the expansion buildings for Stern Trucking & Shipping in St John, Canada.

He sat there looking at it, sipping the 'tonic water.' Leaning back in the chair, he could hear the drone of a diesel truck engine idling below his window, and he drifted off into a memory of another time when this type of work would have held some genuine interest.

Pursing his lips, he was having a conversation with himself in his head: "She just can't help herself. She thinks she has to manage me, always telling me where to be, when, and what clothes to wear."

It was not always like this. Robert never took more than a passing interest in his appearance until they met. After their first date, she started to influence him. First, she made a gentle suggestion about his shirts, and as their relationship grew, so did her suggestions. It started with a plaid shirt, then a sweater with a bold design. "Come on, Robert, just try it on!" He was now smiling to himself, and as aggravating her organizing could be, as he recalled those early years, the memory created a warm glow.

His mind turned to summer and getting his little wooden sailboat ready for the season and out on the water. He took another sip from his glass as he enjoyed the recollection of being out on the lake with the boys on a warm summer day, a gentle breeze like an unseen hand pushing them along.

The office door swung open, and Caroline burst into his office. She brought with her the cold air in from outside. Robert's bubble was abruptly broken. There was a dark cloud over her. She was pale and drawn, eyebrows furrowed, with an angry, pinched look.

"Robert, as if we don't have enough bad stuff going on," glancing at his half-empty glass on the desk, "now you have to start drinking again. I need your support. What is wrong with you?"

Robert jumped out of his daydream and put the pencil to the rendering of the new building before he could say anything, "You were supposed to be at the meeting this morning! We discussed this; you agreed to be there." Robert seemed lost in thought.

Caroline repeated herself and was now almost shouting. "Oh, right, err," and with that lost little boy look on his face, tapping the drawing in front of him, "I got involved in some ideas for the lobby and lost track of time."

Caroline knew he was making excuses. To Robert, it was just like he had been caught with his hand in the cookie jar, but worse. He held his breath, fighting the pent-up frustration that constantly nagged him. His life always seemed to follow the direction of other people. His education, work, marriage, and kids seemed to be a natural progression over which he had little or no control.

At other times, the 'little boy look' captivated her. He had blue eyes with fine lines spread from the corners as if he were about to break into a smile. When they first met, Robert's eyes first drew Caroline in. She was in love with him almost from the start. He was swept off his feet by this young woman whose presence made him feel like the most important person on the planet.

"Every time I think the drinking is over and you are being responsible, it all goes wrong." She pulled the visitor chair towards her as if she was about to sit down and held him in her glare, almost spitting out the words, "When is this going to stop Robert? When?" Every time I turn around to look for you, you are not there!"

Robert was sitting stunned and in silence. Caroline did not wait for him to answer.

"It's because you are drunk again. Why am I not surprised!" Robert began to raise his hands to defend himself but gave up. "Please, Robert, tell me we will not have to go through this again. Now of all time"! Pointing at the bottle, "I can't do this again, and I won't!" She struggled to control her emotions as a tear rolled onto her cheek. She took a deep breath and regained control of herself.

Robert stood up and moved to the side of the desk where Caroline was standing. He tried to put his arms around her. "I am sorry, I am. I will go to AA again."

She pushed him away. "Don't, no, don't, that is not what I need right now. I need your support, and if you can't give that to me, then well…" she trailed off, not wanting to make real her fear of losing someone else she loved.

Caroline sat down, and Robert returned to his chair with just the end of the desk, a corner, between them. It may just have well been an ocean.

"OK, I get it." Robert interrupted her, "I promise I can stop drinking. Do you think I like this? I always think a small one can't hurt, but it does. I have a drink and then feel remorse."

"Fuck you, Robert." She cut in, taking a deep breath, and with a certain intensity, "This is not about you. I don't want to hear about your self-pitying remorse. I want you to think about your family, me, and." Caroline held open her palms and moved them up and down as she emphasized every word, "We must get through this. Stop drinking and help me. Please, Robert, the most important thing right now is that we find out what has happened to Dad."

Robert was only half listening. His demons were clawing at him, just out of reach in the shadows. He waited, knowing there was no point in trying to stop her. He mostly tuned her out, only half listening. Her message was always the same, 'stop drinking and pull yourself together.' For Robert, it wasn't that easy to pull himself together. Every day was a battle between yesterday and tomorrow.

Now calming down, Caroline crossed her arms to protect her inner self while still holding him in her gaze,

"The board and the banks are putting pressure on me. They want me to file some paper that makes Dad dead. They want me to make decisions in his absence. They're also talking about selling. But Dad was in a discussion about merging. I don't know what to do." She fought back the tears that came to her eyes, brushing them away with the back of her hand. Her voice breaking ever so slightly, "They want me to, at least, start thinking about it."

Robert reached out to touch her hand across the desk. She pulled away. He had given up trying to answer her questions sensibly. Figuring there was no point, he just sat back in his chair, waiting for her to calm down.

Caroline, now more gently and composed. "It was hard to sit in that meeting. They are telling me that if Dad doesn't show up and we can't find out what happened to him, we will have to decide how to proceed. But I want to put everything on hold for now. I want to wait, maybe a few more days, before doing anything radical."

Robert was trying to focus but was having difficulty. His hand gradually moved towards the glass with the vodka tonic on his desk. He caught himself and pulled back. "Radical? What kind of radical?"

"I don't know, re-structuring, which could mean many things, but the only thing I can think about now is Dad.

I'm scared about what may have happened to him."

Robert said, "Have we heard anything more from the police?" She shrugged, "The police are nowhere close to knowing what happened. I spoke to Sgt. Hope this morning." Her emotions got the better of her again.

"All you can do is sit there trying to pacify me with that pencil in one hand and a glass of vodka at your elbow."

Robert took a breath and waited a few seconds, and ignoring her comment, he asked very carefully, "So...what do you want to do? Maybe a change could be the right thing just now? Considering a re-structure or even selling may not be a bad idea. Our family: you, the kids, us, are what is important." Waving his arm across the room, he said, "None of this is more important than family right now."

Caroline exploded, "What do you mean, none of this?" She mimicked his hand gesture, waving across the room and standing up. Almost spitting the words out at Robert, "All this is my dad's life work! If you value your family and your life, you will put a cap on that bottle and never open it again."

"No, no." Robert tried to interrupt her. "That's not what I meant."

Caroline stood up and headed to the door. "What use are you! I will get this done without you," pointing to the window, "Maybe if you have time between drinks, you can get someone to repair that goddamned broken gutter; it's been leaking for weeks." The door slammed shut behind her, her words hanging like a sour smell in a stuffy room.

Robert sat there, motionless and numb. He could usually shrug off her tirades with another drink and not let her get to him. But, with Henry missing, it now seemed different. Staring at the door, Robert remained in the chair. Both his hands gripped the edge of the desk. His mouth was slightly open.

He waited for the air to settle, stood up, and returned to the closet at the other end of the room with the half-empty glass in his hand. He opened the bottle, took a swig, added a couple of shots to the glass, and filled it with tonic water.

Stopping at the window on his way back to the desk, he stared out across the yard and into the distance, imagining a future without Caroline and the pain of seeing his children every other weekend and holidays. It would be yet another downward spiral into an abyss.

In his mind, Caroline was the bad one, threatening their marriage and always taking him to task. Their conversation was, in his head, always the same: critical of what he did or did not do. He blamed her for making matters worse, telling himself it couldn't be that bad and that she was making mountains out of molehills. He had convinced himself it was not as bad as she made out. His internal conversations were, in his mind, replays of whatever she said. So, he would have another drink to dull the pain and find a way to blame, if not Caroline, somebody else. And as long as he did, the ill-defined pain he experienced in his body would continue. In his heart of hearts, whatever his problem was, he knew alcohol was not the solution. But still, he continued to drink, even though the thought of losing his marriage and family was a chilling nightmare for him.

He was still in love with Caroline or told himself he was, but lately, his desire had diminished. He knows it's the drinking and accepts that he drinks too often. But to be accused of being drunk, he does not recognize it and is not how he sees himself. He had lost count of how many times in the past couple of years he'd disappointed his two older boys, Mike and Richard, and his daughter Melissa, who would turn twelve this year.

He always tried to be present with them, but some of those precious growing years had been lost. There were the lost softball games, lost last night of the school play, and lost ski trips. He had lost too much family time to the bottom of a vodka bottle.

He turned from the window, returned to his desk, and

sat down. Taking another sip of his drink, Robert picked up a red pencil and started to mark changes to the rendering on the desk. His mind drifted, and almost in an altered state, he wrote in big letters on the drawing, where is Henry anyway? Robert studied it briefly and threw the pencil across the room. He finished the vodka tonic, took his coat and hat from the closet, and left.

Into the Lion's Den

The drive from the offices of Stern Trucking and Shipping in Portland's Old Port to Henry's house on Cape Elizabeth took about fifteen minutes. It was late afternoon, and Caroline was driving. Robert was in the passenger seat next to her. She was still angry with him. However, he had agreed to go and take another look around her dad's house, even though he thought it was a waste of time.

The atmosphere in the car was tense and awkward. Caroline was still mad at Robert for drinking and forgetting about the morning meeting. While trying to put the spat behind her, she was still angry. She was to the point of preventing Robert from driving with any of her children, scared knowing he would probably have been drunk.

Caroline eased the gas, and the car slowed as she approached the low stone wall. She turned the dark blue Volvo left through the open gate and stopped a few yards from the front entrance. Caroline had spent most of her childhood years here, at least those years she could remember, and loved the house and treasured the memories it held, especially of her mother, who died years ago. It still felt to her like the family home.

Henry had thought of selling the house after his wife died. It was too large for him. But he did not sell because, in his heart of hearts, he never had any serious intention to do it.

The shrubs and trees were in their winter sleep, and the rain from earlier had stopped. The dreary cloud-covered sky from this morning had reluctantly given way to sunshine, now beginning to peek from behind the clouds. Despite the warmer-than-usual February weather, the rain was insufficient to melt the snow, and it made a stark contrast with the blue ocean out and beyond the expansive gardens.

The enormous storm, which took everyone by surprise, had now passed. It moved faster than anticipated and was the biggest of the winter. It blanketed the Northeast from Portland to the Canadian Maritimes.

The house had a grand entrance. The front porch, framed by elegant balustrades and a round arch, the entrance seemingly opened its arms and welcomed you to a solid wood door. Shrubs surround the stone-built house, and vines creep around the edges of the wood-framed windows. Nanny berry, honeysuckle, and rhododendron were all waiting for Spring. With Robert beside her, Caroline searched for the house key in an oversized soft leather bag. It functioned as a briefcase with a couple of manila folders containing documents requiring attention. And it was a mom's bag; with three kids, you never know what may be needed. Hidden in its depths were a little fold-up grocery bag, a make-up bag, a Swiss army knife, tissues, a couple of band- aids, and a little pocket for her keys inside. Which was mainly not used, as she often just tossed her keys and whatever else she had in her hand into the bag's hidden depths.

Unlocking the door, she went in, followed by Robert. They stood in the elegant fifteen-foot-wide entrance hall, which led to a wide stairway straight ahead, which gently curved as it led upstairs. The downstairs reception and living rooms were to the right, and to the left, a wide hallway, more like a room, led to the kitchen and Henry's den.

Robert broke the ice, turned to Caroline, and said, "I'll make coffee, and then we can take another look around."

They removed their coats, hats, gloves, and scarves and piled them onto a half-round table with a mirror above and a fat white rotund vase with a handle.

Caroline put one hand on Robert's shoulder and unzipped her boots. It was a sort of peace signal. Robert understood and kicked off his winter boots. As they walked in stocking feet towards the kitchen, he turned over his shoulder and said, "I doubt there's any cream; we'll have to take it back."

Nodding in agreement, she forced a tiny smile around her lips. But she said nothing. She still loved Robert and silently admonished herself for being tough on him, but she told herself he needed someone to keep him away from the vodka, even though no matter how she tried to keep him away from the vodka, it was not working.

Caroline pulled herself onto a high stool at the kitchen counter as Robert took a can of coffee from the fridge, filled the coffee machine, and pressed the button. The smell of fresh-brewed coffee soon filled the air, and with it, a sense of normal.

Robert looked at Caroline. "I know I should have been there with you this morning, and I know how important it was. You needed somebody on your team. I understand, and even though I don't usually get involved in the business, this is different. Just being there would have been the right thing to do. I'm so very sorry, Caroline."

She reached out across the countertop and touched his hand. "OK, apology accepted."

Robert put his hand on hers. "And you know," he continued, "I constantly feel a sense of loss with Henry not being here. When the phone rings, I think maybe it's him, or perhaps you, calling to let me know Henry is safe. He is absent, yet somehow, he is still here."

Caroline nodded, "Yes, I know that feeling," she said. "And we must keep hoping. Yet, not knowing is so upsetting and cruel. If something bad has happened to Dad," she paused and fought a small choke in the back of her throat, "And if he is dead, then I want to know because the uncertainty is killing me." Robert nodded his head.

Then there was silence between them—the kind of silence long-married couples often share. Robert released Caroline's hand and stood up straight. "Let's go over everything we know. Even though the police did look around, they were not looking for anything in particular. "Nothing out of place," they said.

Caroline picked up the coffee cup, gently blew across the top of the coffee, and took a sip. "They seemed to think he would show up having taken a vacation or something and forgot to tell anyone. It's absurd. He would never do that. I told them he had too many responsibilities to go somewhere without telling anyone. Anyone could see that Dad has a busy life, and there is no way he would go anywhere without informing us. Jenny always knows his schedule. No, I don't accept that at all!"

Robert moved to Caroline's side. "Maybe we will find something in the house that helps somehow." He opened a drawer on the cabinet to his right and picked up a pen and pad of paper. Both were imprinted, giveaways advertising a hotel.

"A few days before he disappeared, Dad seemed to be a bit tense and complained about the board putting pressure on him to make decisions. He did say that he was still considering his options and told me he was not yet comfortable with the expansion. He said more work was needed and didn't think he was ready to take the next step. Dad was uncertain if he should sell or merge, and I think that is what he wanted to talk about over breakfast. But he didn't show up, and we still don't know where he is."

Robert suggested, "Perhaps he was thinking about change. Now you are getting involved again, and maybe he thinks it's time for you to take more on. But that has nothing to do with him disappearing like this.

"True," Caroline responded. "But anyway, I know he is ready to change some things. We have talked about it, but nothing firm. He told me the idea of going public had some attractions, but he didn't know if it was possible. He said he was concerned about being in the public eye and would be 'open to scrutiny.' Dad did confide in me and once said, 'There were certain things in his life that should stay private.' I was never able to take the conversation further than that. Staying private seemed attractive even though the expansion is probably necessary."

Robert made a note on the pad:

Maybe time to make some changes.

Pressure from the board.

Going public, yes, or no?

Merge or sell?

Caroline reached to the floor and picked up her bag. "I don't know why he was going to Boston, and the note he left just said he would call in the morning, and it is not like him just to go off somewhere."

Robert said, "He seemed distracted and slightly hostile to me last Thursday. Nothing too unusual in that, I guess. He never really confides anything to me."

"Oh, come on, Robert, he likes you."

"I am not so sure about that, but we have learned to put up with each other over the years. But anyway, come to think of it, Henry seemed to be on the verge of telling me something a few weeks ago but then went quiet and changed the subject."

In agreement, Caroline nodded and said, "He has not spoken to David." She looked up at Robert. "David told me that he had not heard from him in the past couple of weeks, and Dad had not been to bridge night for about three months. He's as worried as we are."

Caroline's Godfather, David J. Preston, had been friends with Henry Stern most of their lives. They met when both were in the services together, and Caroline knew him as Uncle Dave. He was never married and got involved in politics. He was now one of Maine's Senators. Henry's friendship with David Preston had served them both well. David went about his work representing Maine and fighting for what he believed in. Henry supported his efforts and was a regular contributor to the Republicans and a fundraiser for David.

* * *

Robert made a few more notes on the pad and said, "Too bad the plane is down for service. If he had flown, we would've better understood where he was. You know, with flight plans and all that."

Getting up from the kitchen chair, Caroline went to the dining nook's bay window, picking up a small round dish to use as an ashtray. Turning to Robert, "I don't understand why he didn't tell me where he was going, assuming he was going somewhere willingly."

Robert quickly added, "I don't think it's likely, but really, do you think someone may have forced him to go somewhere?"

Caroline was now back at the kitchen counter." I know the police are not ruling out the idea; anything is possible. Suppose he was forced to go somewhere, but somehow, I doubt it. No, my best guess is something happened on his way to Boston, and I am sure he would have told me if he were planning to go somewhere else."

Robert, with a furrowed brow, "Yes, I guess."

"Caroline said, "Right, and in any case, Jenny always knows where he is." She leaned over and picked up the list.

Caroline considered the small details of life, looking for gaps that would illuminate and give a clue as to where Henry could be.

Looking up, she told Robert, "If it were something important, he would have told me. I wonder why he didn't just call and cancel breakfast. Why didn't he call me? Robert, I get scared the more I think about it. Suppose he was forced to go somewhere?"

Our lives are full of mundane things that require attention every day. We behave like King Neptune, trying to hold back the tide. We work on our gardens, maintain the car, shop for groceries, dust shelves, put the dishes in the dishwasher, and so on.

Then something extraordinary happens, and everything normal disappears. All those mundane daily chores that take so much time and attention now have a new significance. Was anything not in its proper place? Was there food in the fridge? Was the laundry done? What time was the appointment? In what way was the routine different?

Caroline and Robert were trying to piece things together and find answers to their many questions. Robert said, "That lunch last Thursday was the last time I saw Henry."

Caroline said, "I thought you saw him at the office on Monday?" You were going to discuss the new office design?"

Robert looked chastened. "Err," he hesitated. "I missed the meeting."

The atmosphere became tense, and as Caroline looked at Robert, her mood changed. She squinted as she looked at him, taking his measure. Once again, there was a shadow on her face. "I was skiing with the kids at the condo and couldn't make it back."

Pursing her lips with her head slightly to one side, she said, "Oh, right, sorry, I forgot." Then, more ferociously, she tried to contain it, but it popped out. "I can guess why you couldn't make it back!" She opened the pack of cigarettes she had placed on the countertop in front of her.

"Do you have to do that?" Robert said. "You know Henry doesn't like smoke in the house."

She lit a cigarette and looked Robert straight in the

eye, daring him to say another word about the habit she could not kick.

Her voice loaded with accusation,

"You didn't wake up in time, did you? And why was that, Robert?" You were supposed to meet Dad at 10, and if you didn't have a hangover, that would give you plenty of time to get back from Sugar Loaf!" Her admonishment was delivered like a well-aimed bullet. She knew she was being defensive about smoking. Robert, not wanting to be drawn into another fight about his drinking, said nothing.

She looked at Robert and held him in her gaze. "I will make a deal. You stop drinking, and I will quit smoking, period!" I do understand. I know that it is hard to give up an addiction, but you must do it."

Robert responded, "Let's not get into this again now. I suggest we look in all the rooms first, see if anything stands out."

For the next hour, they went through drawers in the living rooms, kitchen, dining room, bedrooms, bedside cabinets, and closets, having no idea what they expected to find.

They went into Henry's bedroom. There was a king-size bed, a large window looking out to Casco Bay, and a couple of chairs to sit and take in the morning sun. The room had a feminine feel, still furnished the way Henry's wife had chosen. Robert went into the bathroom as Caroline headed towards the dressing room. She touched her dad's jackets, neatly lined up on the hangers, and the shelves with shirts, sweaters, and more rails with outer coats. She opened drawers and closed them, unsure exactly what she was doing or looking for.

Robert, meanwhile, was in the bathroom looking around. He opened the bathroom cabinet without really taking anything in, closed it, looked at himself in the mirror above the vanity, and pinched the bridge of his nose. Taking another look at himself, Robert ran his fingers down his cheeks as if trying to smooth the lines away. He picked up a book about the history of aviation that was sitting on the vanity. He carelessly flicked through the pages when a photo of a woman fell out. The woman, perhaps in her late forties or early fifties, was well-dressed and posing for the camera. He thought she looked like she was going to a celebration, maybe a wedding or birthday party. On the back, there was a note.

'*My dearest Henry, I will never forget what you did for me. You will be in my heart forever.*' He put the book down, and with the photo in his hand, still half looking at it, he wandered back into Henry's bedroom,

Caroline was coming out of the dressing room. "Here, take a look at this." offering the photo to her. "Do you recognize her?" She took the picture from Robert's outstretched hand and sat in a chair by the window. Robert followed her and sat on the end of the bed facing her.

"I've never seen her and have no idea who she is. It's been more than ten years since Mom died, so it wouldn't surprise me if, well, you know. It's none of our business."

"Yes, maybe. Under normal circumstances, I would agree. But to get any idea as to what, if anything, has happened to Henry, we should explore every angle.

Caroline agreed as she looked again at the photo. She turned it over and read the note on the back. Staring at it, she again turned it over to study the woman's picture. "I don't know, Robert, something about this, and I'm not sure?" Caroline shrugged.

Robert responded, "Maybe it's just an old photo."

Caroline picked up her bag and the pack of cigarettes from the bed next to Robert. He took the photo from Caroline, and they left the bedroom and went downstairs into the hallway. Turning right at the bottom of the stairs, they opened the heavy oak door and entered what felt like a forbidden place. Caroline's Mom had decorated the rest of the house, and Henry's study was the one concession she had made to his choice of furnishings. The family gently teased him and called it 'The Lion's Den.'

The Lion's Den had paneled floor-to-ceiling walls with elegant, traditional, and masculine crown molding. The shelves that lined the walls had books, family photos, some stones collected from a nearby beach, and an assortment of treasures given mainly by friends and family.

We all have these things in our lives. We put them on display as reminders of the ones we love. When holding them, they help us relive an experience or an event that marks the passage of time. They have intrinsic value and are hard to throw away. We tuck some away in drawers and boxes, forgotten until one day we stumble upon something, and the memories of the people and places come flooding back.

The 'Lion's Den' had windows with views across the snow-covered lawn to the ocean, Cushing Island, and beyond. In front of one window was a desk with a leather chair, and to the left was an oversized, upholstered, comfy chair. Caroline picked up a cushion from the floor and placed it back on the chair where it belonged, putting things in order.

She briefly thought about the day the police were there looking around. She mused that Sergeant Hope had tried to reassure her – give her hope. They had looked around, opened drawers, listened to the answering machine, and asked about Henry's usual schedule.

Caroline stood and stared, not touching anything, looking at the desk lamp, the writing pad, some newspapers, and a glass paperweight with a snow scene captured in glass. It snows when you turn it upside down. She gave it to him when he returned from the war when she was nine; that was another time in another house. But through the years, Henry always kept it on his desk. Carelessly, she flicked through neatly stacked papers, looked through drawers, opened files, and shifted things around.

Robert put the photo of the unknown woman on the desk and turned his attention to the bookshelf. Browsing along the row of books, he distractedly ran his hand across the spines as if touching them would somehow, magically, impart what was written, or maybe some unseen force would guide him to the 'right' book. Thoughtlessly, he picked up one about the Second World War. Then, turning to Caroline, "I never thought your dad was interested in the war. He didn't want to talk about it and would only say that it's all in the past and shrug it off."

Caroline had her head in a file and did not respond. Not knowing if she heard or had deliberately ignored him,

Robert shrugged. He was leaning against the bookshelf, and returning his attention to the book, he casually placed one ankle over the other. His eyes were drawn toward a description of the Canadian army's success in liberating Calais in 1943. He began to feel agitated and in need of a drink.

Caroline was looking at a newspaper she had just picked up, the St John Daily News. It had been sitting on the desk under some papers, along with the New York Times and the Boston Globe, which Caroline opened just as Robert was about to suggest they leave.

As she opened the newspaper, a clipping fluttered to the floor. It was from a paper in Quebec, an article about Stern Trucking and Shipping. With it, she found an unsigned note.

'I know I promised never to contact you again, and I would have kept that promise because you saved me from a terrible fate. I owe you, and I will always keep our secrets. But you should know that the 'Marines' are looking for me, and no good can come of it if they ever catch up with me. Please, Henry, come and talk to me. Help me get out of here and away.'

Caroline took a deep breath and looked up at Robert. "What do you make of this?" He closed the book, placed it on the chair, and walked to the desk. Caroline handed him the note, and not waiting for Robert to finish reading, she added, "There is no address given, which means Dad knows where to find this person."

Robert carefully looked at the note and then at Caroline, "What is the date on the newspaper?"

Caroline looked, "It is a couple of weeks before Dad disappeared. Still, it doesn't tell us anything about where he was going when he disappeared or why."

As Caroline closed the newspaper, she noticed some writing in the margin. 'Myrtles Bar, Boston, and the name Frank Lee scrawled next to it. She recognized it as her dad's writing.

Raising her eyebrows and looking at Robert with a half-smile, she held it up triumphantly and pointed. "I don't believe this! Sergeant Hope, who does not offer any, must have missed this. It looks as if Dad was to meet some guy called Frank Lee in Boston. This newspaper is a good lead, Robert, Look! Don't you agree?" Robert sat in the chair beside the desk and said, "Maybe we should let the police have these? We should go home, call the police in the morning and see what they think."

Caroline said, "I am going to Boston to find this, Mr. Lee. If Dad was going there to speak to him, I want to find out what happened. If they met, I need to know what they talked about." Robert stood up and put everything back on the desk next to the photo he had retrieved earlier from the bathroom. "That is absurd! What makes you think you can go to some Boston bar and miraculously run into Mr. Frank Lee? Or what do you expect to find him sitting at a bar waiting for you?"

He was on a roll, pushing back against Caroline. Sometimes, it worked, and he could talk her down from doing something headstrong or foolish. "And what about Canada? How do you know he is not there?"

Caroline picked up the newspaper with the scrawled note and the photo. She took the clipping from Robert's hand and put them in her bag. "I may have to go to Canada, but Boston is closer, so that is where I'll start. I can't just sit around waiting for the police to do something. To them, Dad's just another missing person. Not good enough!" she asserted.

Robert had that helpless look about him, knitting his eyebrows. He took a more conciliatory approach.

"Fine, if your mind is made up, I should come with you – if you want me to?"

"No," Caroline abruptly responded. "You stay here, and I will call Em. I am sure she will come with me."

Emily Whitt was Caroline's best friend and confidant.

"Anyway, we have kids to think about, and this is a trying time for them, and one of us should be here."

As they walked silently to the car, Robert was secretly relieved, but he protested and said, "If you think this is important, we should both go."

Caroline said, "No, I will call Em when we get home."

Robert was not feeling so good, and his body was beginning to crave a shot of vodka. As they got in the car, he made another weak attempt to convince her. "You don't have to do this. We should talk to the police about what we found and let them chase up any leads. It's their job," he emphasized.

His head was splitting. He fastened the seat belt, and for some reason, his mind wandered back to Henry's book on World War Two. "Maybe we should come back tomorrow and look around again?" he suggested. Caroline was quick to respond.

"Tomorrow, I am going to Boston."

Train To Boston

From the loudspeaker came the announcement, "Platform two, the ten o'clock to Boston." It was followed by the screech of the conductor's whistle and the familiar call, "All aboard!" The train began its painful effort to get going. Caroline sat alone in the long carriage, eyes darting out the window, searching. The door facing Caroline at the end of the carriage opened.

She smiled and waved, and as Em got within earshot, she said, "Oh, thank God, Em. I thought you wouldn't make it."

Emily Whitt dropped her overnight bag on the floor and flopped into the seat next to Caroline. The bag was followed by a soft woolen pink hat, which she threw on the seat across from them, along with her black wool gloves with little red hearts on the back. Her hair was black and cut short. Em and Caroline have been friends since junior high school. They grew up together and knew each other's secrets, including all the details of Em's romances. They never really lasted, and she never married. Em would always say, "Why bother!"

Opening a fresh pack of cigarettes, she offered one to Caroline, who refused with a shake of her head. Em took a gold-plated lighter from the pocket of her tailored coat, lit her cigarette, and blew the smoke across the aisle towards an empty seat.

Caroline immediately noticed the ring on the fourth finger of her right hand. "That's new. Who's it for?"

"A new client in New York. "She held her hand out, fingers slightly in the air. "I have to wear it for a while to see if I like it. Do you love it?" "I do," Caroline genuinely responded.

Em was a talented artist. She used acrylics to paint scenes from around the Maine coast, and she especially liked winter and fall when the thin light made colors more dramatic. She also made expensive and unique jewelry for special clients. It gave her independence, which meant she could make her own schedule. She worked from a studio in the third bedroom of her apartment on the Portland waterfront. Em put her hand down, looked at Caroline, and asked, "How are you doing?"

"It's hard, really hard, Em. I haven't been eating properly," pointing to Em's cigarette, "and smoking more. It's the not knowing, you know?"

Now, changing the mood, Em said, "Now, will you

tell me what this is all about, finally? You first said shopping, and I thought that was a good sign. I'm told it's important to try to continue doing routine stuff, and of course, if shopping was it," and with a smile, "then so be it. But then you said you also had to find somebody. So, what's up?"

Caroline took a cigarette from the pack on top of her bag. Em gave Caroline the lighter she had been turning over and over in her hand. Caroline lit the cigarette and handed the lighter back to Emily. Looking more squarely at Em, Caroline said, "I don't know what to say; I feel sick. I have a constant knot in my stomach. The Board is putting pressure on me to make decisions in Dad's absence, and the police don't seem to have anything. That Sergeant Hope is no hope at all, and Robert, I don't know, is just not much help."

The train was now up to cruising speed, leaving Portland with its houses, construction, and storage yards falling behind. Trees all flashed by, becoming a blur, as the train crossed bridges that spanned highways and rivers as it sped through the rural Maine forests of oak and maple, all waiting for the season to change when, suddenly, life springs back, and things start to grow again.

"So, let's hear more about this mystery man. I assume it's a man, and, by the way, does Robert know you are going to find a man in Boston?" A small smile was on her lips. "Okay, what are we doing, and who will we do it with?"

"Yes, you dolt, it's a man, but not what is running through your trash mind!" Caroline Continued," I am not sure. I have a person's name and a bar to check out, that's all!"

"Come on, Caroline. We've been friends for too long for you to be so vague; what is going on? If you don't tell me, I am getting off at the next station. I can go shopping in Boston some other time."

Caroline opened the oversized bag, pulled out a manila folder, and described what she had. As the train slowed on its approach to Saco Station, the trees, backyards, bridges, and side streets became focused again.

Looking at Em, "I keep having all these questions float through my mind. Questions and no answers. Why would he disappear? Why not call me and let me know he needed to cancel breakfast? We were going to meet at his house. Em, it just doesn't make sense. If there had been an accident, we would know. I keep thinking that somebody must have forced him from the house."

Em moved to the seat across from Caroline and replied, "I doubt that very much. Why? For what reason?"

There was a slight pause, and then Em added, 'Although your dad must have enemies, I hope that is not what has happened."

Caroline straightened her back and sat up, leaning against the back of the seat, "Honestly, I have been expecting a ransom note. At least, that would be something. But nothing. It's killing me!" Caroline choked up again and reached into her bag for another tissue.

The conductor's whistle screamed out, and the train slowly got going and reached cruising speed.

More serious now, Em reached across the carriage to touch Caroline's hands. "You know I am with you all the way. So, what is going on?" Caroline returned her attention to the manila folder just as the door connecting the carriages opened. A porter, unsteadily pushing a food trolley, moved along the carriage and stopped. He looked at both the women. "Coffee, tea, snacks?" Em looked up. I'll take some coffee."

He then looked at Caroline with raised eyebrows, and Caroline replied with a nod, "Thanks, cream, no sugar."

He handed them the coffee and continued along the carriage to the one other person sitting close to the connecting door at the other end of the carriage.

With their coffee in hand, Caroline showed Em the

newspaper cutting with the story about Stern Trucking and Shipping.

Em read the story, alternating between a sip of coffee and a drag on a cigarette, looked up, and said, "So what? This article is about the possible closing of the warehouse in St. John. You told me that was to make the Unions sit up and take notice?"

"It is, was, but look at this." She handed Em the note she had found at her dad's house yesterday with the newspaper clipping. Em read it aloud.

'I know I promised never to contact you again, and I would have kept that promise because you saved me from a terrible fate. I owe you, and I will always keep our secrets. But you should know the 'Marines' are looking for me. No good can come if they ever catch up with me. Please, Henry, come and talk to me. Help me get out of here and away.'

Em looked up at Caroline and was about to speak, Caroline interrupted her. "Look at the date in the newspaper; it is two weeks before Dad disappeared." Em stubbed out the cigarette in the ashtray built into the arm of the seat, "I don't get it?"

The train slowed as the next station approached, "But this is a Canadian newspaper; we are going in the wrong direction!"

"Look at this, Em; I think the note came from this guy." Caroline handed Emily a folded newspaper page with the note in her dad's recognizable scrawl. Caroline pointed at it and said, "See, Myrtles Bar, Boston, Frank Lee."

With raised eyebrows and a grin, Emily said,

"Are you kidding me, Frank Lee!"

Em and Caroline knew each other's ways. They had inside jokes and a shared penchant for childlike humor and irony. "Frank Lee," Emily giggled and repeated herself, "Frankly, are you kidding me!"

"And Sergeant Hope," Caroline added, "Who does not offer any!" She shook her head from side to side and pressed her lips together in a half smile. Em's gesture matched Caroline's expression, and they found that warm space the two women had shared for years. The cloud surrounding Caroline lifted briefly. Em said, "This Frank Lee guy—I hope he is good-looking.

Are you taking me on a blind date?"

They both laughed, and Caroline smiled and said,

"You never know!"

The air around their heads was now filled with smoke. Emily got up and opened the window. She stood looking out onto the platform as half a dozen people boarded the train, slamming the doors behind them. The chilly air wafted in and cleared some smoke from their cigarettes. Caroline pulled her coat around herself as a chill crept over her body, and her mood changed again. The cloud surrounding her returned as the platform master's shrill whistle screamed out, and the train strained as it got going. With the sound of the wheels scraping on the track, Emily closed the window and returned to her seat opposite Caroline. The connecting carriage door opened, and a woman with a young child moved along the aisle, continued past the two women, and sat at the far end of the carriage, well away from the smoke.

Em looked at Caroline, "So are we just to find this bar in Boston and ask for Frank?"

Caroline reached for another cigarette and looked at Em. "OK, I am going to make a pact with you. We have tried many times. Let's make this last pack of cigarettes we will ever buy; I have promised myself time and time again and always fail. And now I am smoking even more. What do you say?"

"Oh, no, not that again!" Shaking her head.

"Do we have to?"

"You know we should, and I keep on at Robert about his drinking when I have a habit I can't quit."

"Ah, right, but I am not married to Robert, thank

God!" Caroline responded with an almost imperceptible shrug, and a slight smile crept around her mouth as she turned her head away from Em and gazed out the window. A few seconds passed in silence. Then Em asked, "Did you ever hear from that investment banker guy again? What was his name?"

Caroline turned to Em, now with a broader smile.

"Douglas Kingsley. But that was two years ago."

"Did he ever get back with his wife?"

"Not as far as I know."

"He was cute," Em said with a smile.

"He lived in Boston, right?

Remembering how tortured she had been, Caroline let out a sigh. She had been unfaithful to Robert. Em, who thought every married woman should have at least one good affair before reaching the ripe old age of forty, had encouraged her. She would tell Caroline, "You may never get back with Robert, and anyway, you only have one life, and this is the nineteen seventies, not the eighteen hundred!"

Reflections in a Window

They met in Henry's office about two years ago. Robert was in the hospital, trying to recover from too much alcohol, and Caroline was seriously considering divorce. While she still loved him, and they married for better or worse, Robert's drinking drove them apart. Caroline was with her dad at Stern Trucking and Shipping offices for a monthly board meeting. Henry walked him out the door as Caroline was about to go in. He was introduced to Caroline as an investment banker from New York, here to discuss the possibility of a future expansion. There was something about that meeting. It was a fleeting moment, and a feeling had come over her. One not experienced for some years. She had been so busy looking after the kids while Robert was in rehab, and their relationship was barely holding together. Now, as she gazed out the train window, she thought about how romance fades and the work of looking after the love begins. If you don't look after and nurture it, you lose it. It happens to many couples. Over time, an existence settles in. Routines, habits, and expectations all get a place to settle down. It is as if they are independent beings with the sole purpose of making us comfortable. We get numb and accept things as they are. After twenty years, there no longer seems to be any reason to expect things to be different. That is unless something happens, like what happened to Caroline that day.

It was a look, a faint smell of soap, and how he put his head slightly to one side with a shy, 'caught in the headlights' smile. Douglas Kingsley wore a white shirt, red tie, and a dark grey suit with a white handkerchief peeking from the outside breast pocket. He projected self-assured confidence. Their introduction and pleasantries lasted only a minute, and he left the building.

Later, she found a way to ask her dad more about him. He smiled, raised his eyebrows, and teasingly, Henry said, "And you a married woman!" Caroline rolled her eyes, but Henry continued, "I don't know much about him. He works for one of the banks who want our business and to help with any planned future development." That was it. Henry said nothing more about him.

But fate sometimes throws a curve ball. Douglas left a note with his phone number on her car and an apology for the scratch he had made to it as he left the parking lot.

She called him the next day, and they both realized they had met the day before.

"I'll still be in town tomorrow.

Can we meet to exchange information?"

She hesitated.

"Why not just give me the information now."

"I could, but then I would not be able to invite you to lunch as an apology." Caroline felt herself blush as a feeling came over her. It started with a tiny ripple in her tummy, followed by a slight, almost imperceptible warmth that gently washed over her.

In some ways, it was understandable, perhaps forgivable. Robert was in rehab for the second time. She was lonely, feeling isolated, the years ticking by, and looking at turning forty. It was not planned. Em constantly reminded her that she needed to think about getting on with her life and not put up with Robert's nonsense anymore.

Over lunch, the conversation turned to more personal matters. He asked Caroline to call him Doug, and they talked about their history, the movies they liked, and their favorite local restaurants. Doug was forthcoming and seemed comfortable sharing. He was divorced and had two young children, two boys, whom he saw every other weekend. Although he did not say it, Caroline heard him hint that he was lonely and needed someone special. Then Doug said, "There's a concert, and we could have dinner. Would you like to go?"

"You mean like a date?"

He was a bit taken aback by her bluntness. "Well, yes, but if that is a bit unnerving for you, we could invite some other people and enjoy a concert as friends."

With all the seriousness she could gather, Caroline said, "I am married, but you know that, right?" There was a brief silence, and then, "Although a concert would be lovely, honestly, a date? Maybe it would be better to invite others."

Doug replied, "I am only suggesting a concert and perhaps a bite to eat."

Caroline smiled, "Well, if that is all you are thinking, OK. I would enjoy the concert, and getting a break from the routine would be good." However, she had been having fanciful thoughts since they met—nothing explicit, just a passing question that she quickly chased away.

Caroline came out of her revelry and asked, "Em, what do you think I should do if I can't find Frank Lee?"

"What is more important is what you think you should do."

"Em, I asked a straightforward question. You can be so infuriating sometimes!"

"That is why we are friends. You don't scare me."

Turning back to Em, "I am going to have to work on that," she said, smiling. Then, more seriously, "So, you think I should give up the chase."

"I didn't say that; it is not what you will do. I know you too well. You want me to tell you not to bother so you can get all determined and do what you intend to do anyway. No, we will see if we can find this Frank Lee and then find the divorcees". She was smiling.

Caroline, as ever, was seduced by her smile. Em was goofy, and Caroline loved her for it.

Caroline said, "Wish I knew where he was."

Em, with a twinkle in her eye, "Who, the banker?" He lives in Boston, right?"

"Yes, he does, but I was talking about my dad, you idiot!"

They both smiled. Caroline continued, "I have booked us a room at the Copley."

Em said, "Twins, I hope." With a slight shrug of her shoulders, Caroline smiled and joined in the joke, "Of course not!"

The train slowed, and the Conductor announced the imminent arrival in Boston. They picked up their bags and walked along the carriage to the exit.

Cause for Concern

Senator Preston stepped from the plane that had brought him from Maine to Washington. As a Maine Senator, he worked in the Dirksen Building on Pennsylvania Avenue. He was met at the airport by his driver. "Good morning, Senator."

Senator Preston nodded and asked, "How are you, Chris?" Without waiting for an answer, "How are the roads looking? Any jams?"

"No, we should have time to spare for your first meeting." Chris handed him a folder containing the briefing documents he would need while in Washington. "July asked me to give you this. She expects to have clarified some last-minute changes and questions by the time we get to the office."

The drive from the airport took about an hour, giving the senator enough time to review the file and make notes. Opening the office door, July Grey greeted him. She had worked for David since before he was elected. July was tight-lipped, well-organized, and committed to the party. She efficiently and without complaint managed all his day-to-day affairs. She was discreet and kept his secrets. David Preston served in the Second World War.

He was a dedicated public servant with never a whiff of scandal. July was his gatekeeper, and she kept a wall around him, ensuring his public persona. He had a reputation for being a man of the people, dedicated to working on their behalf. He was effective and got things done.

Picking up a red folder, July got up from her desk and greeted him. "Good morning, David. Do you have any news about Henry?"

"Sadly, nothing yet. It is extremely worrying. We should be doing more with the national press despite what Caroline says. But she is reluctant. No doubt we will find him soon. God, I hope so!"

July acknowledged David with a shake of her head as she handed him the folder. "Here is the latest report for the Senate Finance Committee. I highlighted some things you would want to look at. Sorry I couldn't give it to Chris earlier. It wasn't ready last night, and Chris left early this morning from home."

"It's not a problem. I have a few minutes to go over it."

July walked with him into his office. "There is also a list of items on the agenda for the next few days. Do you want coffee?"

"No thanks, July. Let's get to it. Time is pressing."

July said, "Everything is in order. We should deal with 1 through 3; the rest can carry over."

David looked down and focused on the list in front of him. She continued, "I also have your briefing papers for the Chinese Trade Mission, but that can also wait till tomorrow. Oh, and by the way, your flight back to Maine on Thursday had to be changed. The flight will be an hour later. Airline schedules!"

They got through the discussion, and July left the office. David stood at his desk, flicking through papers and getting ready for the Finance Committee Chamber, when July buzzed the intercom phone. "David, Caroline is trying to reach you. Say's It won't take a minute."

David picked up the phone and sat down in the chair. "Hi, Caroline. How are you holding up?"

"Honestly, I am slowly going out of my mind."

David said, "Seriously, Caroline, we should get information out to the press. If you agree, we can get something about his disappearance on the national evening news."

"Maybe you are right," she replied. "I've been thinking about it, and Sergeant Hope has also been pressing me on that. I'm just not sure. I know it gives us a better chance of finding somebody who can help. But I still think it could seriously damage the company at this crucial time, and to say he is lost, missing, well...."

David interrupted her. "I think it is time to see if we can get national coverage. Somebody must know something about where he is. Yes, it may cause some damage, but we can manage it. Your dad is more important than the company. If you agree, I'll take care of it. I think it's a mistake to wait any longer. It's been too long, and anyone important to Stern already knows, so let's proceed. Do you agree?"

Caroline suggested, "Well, if we are going to do it, I assume you would include Boston. And where else?"

"What, yes, of course, the Boston news along with Portland, Augusta, along the coast to Bar Harbor, and the local papers in Canada.

Caroline said, "I am in Boston now."

"What's that, Caroline? Why?"

She started to explain about Mr. Lee. David listened for a few minutes and then interrupted her, "Caroline, I don't think it is a good idea for you to be chasing all over the place looking for people you know nothing about or if they have any connection to Henry."

Caroline said, "I know it's a long shot, but at least it's something I can do. I feel so helpless most of the time. I am going to start at Myrtles Bar. It is just a few blocks from the Hotel."

"What?" David asked but did not wait for an answer. He heard what she said. "How would you expect to go to a bar and find somebody you have never met? What makes you think you can find him? All you have is a note found on your dad's desk." David looked at his watch and took a deep breath, trying to calm his concerns. "You never know what stones you may be turning over."

"What do you mean?"

He hesitated slightly, "I am as worried as you, of course…." Caroline interrupted, "Well, I also have this photo of a woman with a note to Dad on the back thanking him for some help he gave her."

David, now clearly concerned, "Photo of who?"

"I have no idea. She looks pleasant, but there is something about her photo, and I am unsure what it is. She looks sad. When Robert first showed the photo to me, I did not recognize her. But since then, I have a feeling I know her from somewhere, but, oh, I don't know, it may just be my imagination."

"Mmm, well, Henry may have been many things, but

he was not a philanderer. I know that for sure he was faithful to your mom."

"Yes, and of course, I was not suggesting that. And even if he was, who are we to judge? But just so you know, some hints on what we found suggest I may have to go to Canada, probably to the terminal at St John, especially if Boston turns out to be a bust."

"Canada? Caroline, why on earth?"

She replied, "Robert and I found a note among the papers on Dad's desk and an article about the St John terminal. Someone must have sent it to him for a reason because he had already seen that article weeks ago, but I would not know where to start, so for now, I am in Boston."

David tried to get her to give up the chase. "My advice is just to let the police do their job." He paused. "What makes you think there are answers to his whereabouts in Boston, or if it comes to it, Canada? "

Caroline replied, somewhat dryly, "I just do, and I can't sit around and do nothing. I have to try."

Sensing there was no point in resisting more and not wanting to go further down a conversational rabbit hole, David replied, "Well, I guess your mind is made up?" She did not respond. "Call me later and let me know if you need anything." He was about to hang up. "Oh, and by the way, I am coming to Portland this weekend and think we should talk. Let's go over everything and see what else we can do."

"OK, I will have lunch ready at home."

David replied, "Yes, thanks. That would be good. We need to plan where to go next with this. My advice would be to go home, but I know you won't. So good luck anyway, say hi to Emily, and please take care."

* * *

Senator Preston put the phone down and stared off into the distance. He looked at his watch. Time was pressing. He had just a few minutes before having to leave the office for the meeting. He picked up the phone and punched the numbers on the keypad to an unlisted phone number, one he had committed to memory.

"It's Preston. I have a job for you. Get yourself to Boston now, and I will call you later. No, not now. I am running late. I want you to go to the Copley Plaza Hotel, get a room, and wait for my call." The voice on the other end started to ask questions. "Listen, just do it. I will tell you more later."

He put the phone down and gazed blankly at it, his eyebrows knitted together and his lips slightly pursed. He took a deep breath and let it out gently as he counted to ten. He had to prevent things from getting out of hand and going beyond where they needed to go.

* * *

Following the conversation with her godfather, Caroline put the phone down and turned to Em, who was mindlessly browsing through a magazine with one ear on Caroline's conversation with David. "Anything new?"

"No, we agreed to step things up with the press."

Em replied, "Yes, I heard, and I think he is right."

"I guess. David seems alarmed that we were here, but I suppose it's understandable."

Em said, "I am getting hungry, and if we are ever going to have a nose around that bar and put this wild goose chase to rest, then we should probably go there sooner rather than later. We can ask for Mr. Lee, and when we are told nobody knows him, we can have a nice dinner. Then, tomorrow, a few hours of shopping before heading home.

Caroline furrowed her eyebrows and looked at Em. She was glad Em was here with her.

Red Wine and Fajitas

It was snowing as they walked the two blocks from the hotel to Myrtles Bar. Stamping the snow from their feet, Caroline and Em entered a decent replica of a pub one would expect to find in Dublin. The lights were not too bright, and small tables with beer mats under glass and fancy ironwork legs were dotted around the room. Over to one side, some private booths were decked out in red leather, now slightly worn from years of people sliding in and out across the seat.

Caroline and Em were happy to get inside out of the weather. They briefly looked around and then went to the bar. The Bartender immediately caught their eye and asked, "What would you like?" They each ordered a glass of red wine, took out their cigarettes, lit up, and blew smoke in the air above their heads. Looking sideways at Em, Caroline said,

"Make the most of it. We quit soon!"

"Ah, that again," Em complained.

The bartender brought their wine. They sat for a while, and after a minute or two, he engaged them in conversation.

"How is that Merlot?" With a nod of their heads in agreement, "Good." "Yes, Californian. People seem to like it. Are you visiting, or do you live here?"

Both responded, "No." EM added,

"Just visiting from Portland. We are on a mission."

The bartender smiled. "A secret mission!"

Caroline smiled and said, "No, not a secret, but let me ask you something. I think you may know my dad. He frequently comes to Boston on business and often drops by for a whisky. Henry Stern, Does the name ring a bell?"

"No, sorry, it doesn't. But we get many people coming and going."

Interrupting, Caroline described her dad and mentioned Stern Trucking and Shipping.

The Bartender, appearing to give the question serious thought, "No, don't know that I know him."

"Well, we are looking for somebody else as well. Frank Lee." The Bartender turned his head sideways a little and squinted his eyes.

"Do you know Frank? He hasn't been around for a while."

Caroline's tummy was churning. Em swallowed her glass of wine and asked for another. The barman poured and offered one to Caroline, who declined, having hardly touched her drink.

"I don't know the man. I found his note to my dad, who has gone missing."

The barman now sounded concerned.

"Your Dad, he's missing?" Caroline replied,

"Yes, he was supposed to meet Frank here, but as far as we know, he never showed up." Caroline began to tear up. She sensed a glimmer of hope but was stumbling in the dark and hated it. Em lit another cigarette.

More people came into the bar. The barman turned his attention to other customers. Caroline and Em looked at each other with mouths wide open.

Em said, "What!" Her mind was racing, and Caroline took a gulp of her wine without thinking about what she was drinking. "I knew it, Em. I knew it in my gut. This Frank guy knows something."

"You don't know that, but he knows your dad. We knew that before we came here. The question now is, how do we find him?" The barman returned, having served the new arrivals. He picked up where he had left off. "I have not seen Frank for about two weeks. Funny, though, there was someone here looking for him last week, and he said they were old friends from the war, you know, World War Two."

Em asked, "Did he give his name?"

"No, he had a quick drink and left. The only reason I remember him is that I'd been wondering about Franky. I haven't seen him for a while and have been wondering if he was OK".

Em put $10 on the bar. "What can you tell us about Frank Lee." The barman picked it up with a quick thank you and put it in his pocket.

"All I can tell you is that he is a street vendor. He works a hot dog stand out there." He pointed to the street. "He's usually out there every day, mostly in the summer and the winter at lunchtime if it is not too cold or snowy. His name is a bit of a joke around here. Frank Lee, franks, and hot dogs, see? He has an accent. French, I think. He mostly keeps to himself. Frank comes in to use the bathroom and maybe chats about the weather and the Red Sox, but nothing much. Most days, he sits there on the corner and has a beer at the end of the day before heading home." Pointing to a couple of seats to the right from where Em was sitting. "Usually, he has one beer before heading out."

Caroline asked, 'What does he look like?"

"He's about five feet six, grey hair. At this time of year, he wears one of those black night watch hats you can pull down over your ears. You know, like a ship's crewman might wear. He has a scar on the back of his right hand. I asked him about it once. He mumbled something about some crazy women in a bar in France during the war."

Caroline asked, "Do you know where he lives?"

"Afraid not. But he keeps his wagon in a yard near the Market. It is a business that mostly attracts 'fly-by-nights' and minor criminals. People living under the radar, guys that like to run a cash business and, well, you know how it is."

Em said, "Well, I am not sure I do," not expecting any other response as the barmen moved to a raised hand at the other end of the bar.

Caroline finished her wine and turned to Em. "Why did Dad come to Boston to meet a hot dog vendor?" She waited a minute while the barman finished pulling a beer and caught his eye. She lifted her glass slightly, "I'll have another, please." He filled her glass and again was distracted by other customers.

"Em, why would Dad agree to meet a man who sells hot dogs on the street? What possible business could he have with him? And who was the other person looking for him?"

Em shrugged, "That's why we are here, right? We will find out with any luck, but I still think it's a long shot."

Their eyes were drawn to the TV fixed above the bar.

It was the roundup of the six o'clock news. The newscaster reported on the usual stuff as pictures flashed onto the screen: financial reports, the war in Vietnam, and veteran issues. There was a brief interview with Richard Nixon and a piece about a woman, an ex-Nazi concentration camp guard who had been found and arrested in Brooklyn. There was also an interview with a representative of the Simon Wiesenthal Organization who had been hunting and prosecuting Nazis since the end of the war. The representative explained how this woman, the ex-Nazi guard, had been hiding in plain sight for years.

Caroline and Em were only half listening as they had other things on their minds. That is until the last item when the newscaster said, "When we come back, more on Henry Stern, the Head of Stern Trucking and Shipping, who is reported missing." The channel then took a station break.

Caroline sat up, nudged Em, and, with a nod, pointed towards the TV. Turning to Em, "Well, that was quick. David knows how to pull strings for sure!" Em got the bartender's attention.

"They have a piece about her dad coming up when the ads are done. Could we turn the sound up for a minute?" He obliged. When the station break was over, a photo of Henry Stern was flashed onto the screen. Caroline said, "See, that's my dad, and we have no idea where he is."

All three watched intently as the newscaster gave a thumbnail sketch of Henry and asked anyone who had seen him to contact the local police. The barman turned to Caroline, "So that's your dad? I do know him." He quickly added, "but only as a customer who comes in from time to time. He was here a couple of weeks back." And thinking about it for a second, "I am pretty sure that the last time he was here, he sat there," looking at the seat next to Caroline. " Now, I am certain. Franky came in and appeared to know your dad. What is this all about?"

Caroline responded. "I wish I knew. We just found a scribbled note with Frank Lee's name and the name of this bar as the place to meet him."

The barman grinned and said, "Now, aren't you a regular Sherlock Holmes? Anyway, they took their drinks and sat together," then pointing, "Over there in the corner." Both Em and Caroline turned to look to where he had pointed." The barman continued, "There was a bit of a commotion, and Frank spilled his beer. The man he was with, your dad if it was him, had to get a cloth and dab his pants off. And thinking about it, that was the last time I saw Franky. I don't think I've seen him since. I figured the weather was stopping him from working, or maybe he could be sick and laying low."

Em said, "If he is sick, somebody needs to check on him. What's the address?"

"As I said, I don't know where he lives, but you can find where he keeps his wagon and stuff easily enough." The barman drew a map on a napkin and said," It will take about ten minutes in a taxi. Frank has a small pickup, a green Ford, to tow the hot dog wagon. So, if you see it outside, you will probably find him around somewhere."

Em looked at her watch and turned to Caroline, "It's too late for us to go there tonight. We could go there tomorrow morning." Then, wistfully, "I guess there goes shopping!"

After thanking the barman at Myrtle's, they left. Wrapping their arms around themselves and with shoulders crunched and heads slightly bent forward, they were in the restaurant within ten minutes. The Southern Border Mexican Restaurant was close to the Boston Public Library and tucked away in a corner with an entrance in a side alley. A bright light under a blue awning greeted them. Once inside the restaurant, the waitress showed them to a table. They removed their coats, hung them on the back of their chairs, settled in, and gave their order to the waiter.

Soon enough, the tacos and fajitas arrived, served on

a sizzling plate. Over dinner, they reviewed what they knew.

They did not see the person across the street who had followed them to the bar, nor when he watched them enter the restaurant. They had no idea someone was watching them from the shadows of a doorway across the alley.

Taking their time over dinner, they explored every detail of what they knew and wished they knew. They finished dinner, stubbed out the last after-dinner cigarettes, retrieved their coats, and prepared to head out into the cold and to the Hotel. Once outside, they took half a dozen steps, and Em stopped.

"Wait, hold on a moment. I left my lighter on the table. I won't be a minute."

She turned and went back into the restaurant. Caroline stood with arms folded across her chest, her bag hooked over her elbow. Suddenly, everything was a blur. She was knocked over, and her bag was snatched from her. She just caught a glimpse of a dark figure running off into the night. '*He*,' she assumed it was a he, turned a corner and was gone. Caroline was struggling to get up as Em came back from the restaurant.

"Are you OK? What happened?"

Caroline was shaking. "I was just mugged. Someone grabbed my bag, knocked me down, and," pointing in the direction where the attacker disappeared around the corner, "ran off down there."

They both went back into the restaurant and spoke to the owner. They described what had happened, and the owner called the police. About ten minutes later, a police cruiser arrived. The officer asked a few questions, made notes, and checked to see if there was anything else he could do. He promised to look around and told her she would have to complete a report at the police station in the morning.

Back in the hotel, Caroline stretched out on the bed with her hands behind her head. She stared at the ceiling, projecting images of what happened as if it were a movie. Turning to Em, sitting on the bed across from her, she said, "I have to believe the mugging was just that. Otherwise, there is no explanation."

Em replied, "That's what I have been telling you. The bartender is the only person who knows you are here and looking for information." She paused, "unless, of course, you want to interrogate David? Or Robert!

"As if! But something is nagging at me in my gut."

The phone rang. Caroline lifted the receiver from the phone on the bedside table. "This is the police station on Tremont Street. Is this Caroline Hall?"

"This is Caroline. Have you caught the person who

robbed me?"

"I am afraid not, but we did find your bag. You can collect it from the station in the morning." Caroline hung up the phone. Em picked up the phone and handed it to Caroline. "You had better call Richard and let him know we are onto something and you are OK."

"Oh shit, I forgot all about calling him in all the excitement." Caroline took the phone from Em and said, "I'm not going to tell him about the mugging, and don't you dare say a word!" Em, with raised eyebrows, gestured as if to pull a zipper on her lips.

At 8:30 the following day, they took a taxi for the ten-minute ride to the Tremont Street Police Headquarters. They completed the report noting the loss of credit cards and money. More importantly for Caroline, the envelope with the note from Frank Lee, the article from the Canadian press, and the photo of the woman with the message on the back were all missing.

Standing outside on the street, the storm from last night had blown by, and the sun was shining. Everything glistened in the morning light. Traffic was light, and snowplows were busy clearing the roads and sidewalks. Em tried to reassure her, but Caroline was distraught and said, "The papers, everything taken. It's too much of a coincidence. Yet another one! Honestly, I think it is sinister!"

"Caroline, don't you think you are being a bit crazy? You were mugged for the money. Let's get the train and go home."

Caroline quickly responded. "I am not giving up now. We should go to where Frank Lee leaves his hot dog wagon, and maybe we can find his address. And I want to talk to the barman again and," waving her hand to a passing taxi, "I am going to find Frank Lee dead or alive, mugged or not. That's it. You can go home if you wish, or we can take a later train or stay another night. Just look on the bright side; if it all comes to nothing, then we still get to go shopping at Filene's!"

Em smiled and shrugged her shoulders. They got into the taxi, mimicking the bartender; Em said, "OK, Sherlock Holmes, let's go."

Finding Frank Lee

Emily paid the driver twenty minutes later, and they stepped from the taxi to the sidewalk. Much of the snow had been cleared, and the gates were open. There were three pick-up trucks in the yard. None of them were green. Caroline and Em stepped to one side, allowing a truck and trailer with four hot dog wagons to exit the gate. Just inside the yard, two guys were peering under the hood of a truck.

"Any of you guys know Frank Lee? Franky," Em called out. Caroline nudged her. "There's no holding you back!"

Em strode towards them, and as they looked up, "Who wants to know?" Em quickly replied with a smile. "His mother!"

"Lady, if you're his mother, then I'm his pops," grinning, "and you know what that means." He laughed at his joke, as did Em. She pursed her lips.

"Yeah, well, I know him. He owes me money. Do you want to pay it on his behalf, or would you prefer to work it off?" He was still smiling as he wiped his hands on a piece of cloth as Caroline caught up with Em.

The second guy became interested and looked up from fiddling with the engine. "You don't seem like the kind of woman he hangs out with. What's up?"

Caroline explained the situation to them. The first man suggested she go inside the office to speak to their boss, Mark, and pointed to a small building about the size of four garden sheds lined up.

They thanked the guys and crossed the yard to the office. The door had a carelessly installed ratty-looking office sign hanging from one remaining supporting nail. They gingerly opened the office door and went in. The place could do with a good scrub. There was a small metal desk with a black push-button phone, a pile of papers, and what looked like yesterday's pizza on a paper plate.

Mark was sitting behind the desk with a newspaper open in front of him. He looked like an ex-heavyweight wrestler, light reflecting from his billiard ball head. He looked up from the newspaper as the two women walked in.

Caroline introduced herself and said, "I hope you can help me. I'm looking for someone. Frank Lee, is he around anywhere?"

"Who wants to know?" he asked guardedly.

Caroline added, "We are trying to find my dad. He was supposed to meet Frank, and now we can't find either of them." And trying to explain more fully, "Well, he was supposed to be meeting my dad. It was on the news yesterday. My dad is Henry Stern. Did you see it?"

"Nah, don't watch the news that much. Too depressing," and before Mark could go off on a rant about how bad the world was, Em said, "You don't happen to have his phone number?"

"Tell me why I should give it to you. I don't know you from Adam." He indicated that they should sit down.

Caroline sat on one of the cheap folding chairs in front of the desk, and Em sat on the other. She looked at Caroline and said, "Let's explain everything."

The next ten minutes were a question-and-answer session, which concluded with Caroline almost begging. "Mark, you are our only hope of finding him. What can you tell us about him? Or at least tell us where he lives. At least we can go and try to find Mr. Lee. You must know where he lives?"

Em says, "Or give us his phone number. Suppose he is ill and needs some help. You would be helping him."

Mark now sat forward in his chair, one elbow on the desk, and thoughtfully rubbed his upper lip with his left hand and index finger.

"His phone number won't do you any good. I tried it

half a dozen times, but no answer. Frank has not been around for a week or so."

"Maybe you can tell us something about him?" Asked Em. "Not really, I can't. Frank is a private guy. But I can tell you he's not a bad person." Nodding his head and pointing his nose to the door with a wry smile. "Well, at least not more than the other 'jailbirds' around here. All I can tell is he's a steady worker, and he's been around here for a while now."

Mark opened a drawer and pulled out a small, dog-eared notebook. He tore a piece of paper from a pad that was sitting under yesterday's pizza and wrote the address and phone number down, handing it to Caroline, "As I said, the phone number won't do you any good, but maybe you can find him at his apartment."

Caroline took the slip of paper, turned to Em, and said, "We are going to find him," and turning back to Mark, "Thank you so much."

Mark smiled, "The address is in Somerville, an apartment. That's all I know about where he lives. His wagon has been sitting here for over a week, and he owes me rent." As Caroline and Em stood up, he added, "If you see him, tell him he needs to let me know what's happening. Somebody else wants to lease his cart." Caroline and Em started to leave and, over their shoulders, assured Mark they would pass the message on.

Outside, Caroline let out a deep breath. "This is great; we have his address. Let's go."

Em said, "And I was hoping for another dead end! Well, there goes shopping." And then, "Are you sure about this, Caroline? Maybe we should tell the police and let them investigate."

"Emily Whitt, do you seriously think we should give up and go home?"

Somewhat grudgingly, Em replied, "No, not really, and even if I did, I can see there is no stopping you now. But we must be careful. No more muggings!"

* * *

The taxi driver found Frank Lee's building and stopped a foot from the snow piled by the plows against the sidewalk. Emily paid and, turning to Caroline, handed her two twenty-dollar bills from her wallet and said, "Since you were robbed and all."

Somerville is a small town, recovering from several years of industrial and population decline, and home to Tufts University. Now divided into apartments that had seen better days, row houses lined the shabby streets. It was quiet, with just a few cars parked here and there; most residents were probably at work. The taxi pulled away as they carefully stepped across a pile of snow. Stale cooking smells greeted them as they entered the small lobby of the apartment building. Em looked at Caroline and pinched her nose between her right thumb and forefinger.

"Pew!" she exclaimed. Caroline wrinkled her nose and screwed up her face.

Apartments A and B were on the ground floor. An overfilled trash can outside apartment A contributed to the general neglect. A sign to apartments B and C pointed them up a narrow, steep flight of stairs with a dusty, worn carpet, discarded chewing gum wrapper, and another overfilled trash can at the top. They climbed the stairs and banged on the door to apartment B. There was no answer. Em turned the doorknob, and to her surprise, the door opened. "Frank," she called out, "Anyone there? Anyone home?" There was no answer.

They entered an apartment that was in chaos. It had been ransacked, and someone was looking for something. Chairs were turned over, and papers carelessly spilled over the floor. "Let's get out of here, Caroline. I don't like the look of this."

Caroline stepped further into the sad little apartment and walked through the living room, past the overturned chairs, and into the kitchen. Em followed her. Like the rest of the building, it was neglected and sorely needed a coat of paint. There was moldy, uneaten food in the pan on the stovetop and a couple of dirty plates on the table. She turned to Em, who was just one step behind her. "It looks as if someone left in a hurry. They didn't finish whatever that is," pointing to the moldy food in the pan, who created this mess. I wonder what they were looking for. I know this has something to do with Dad. I know it."

Em replied, "You don't know that, and it's probably just a coincidence." They returned to the living room, and Em entered the small bedroom. The bed was turned upside down, and clothes spread everywhere. Caroline remained in the living room looking at some papers, bills mostly, and junk mail she had picked up from the floor. Em came back in from the bedroom, and then, the front door to the apartment swung open. Two burly men, both with guns in their hands, rushed them.

"Keep your hands where I can see them, and get down on your knees." They pushed Caroline and Em to the floor.

One of the men quickly checked their coat pockets, and though they tried to fight back, it made no difference. Em and Caroline were picked up off the floor and manhandled into chairs one of the men had set upright. "Now, you two, just sit down and shut up."

They were handcuffed to the chairs, trembling, the blood drained from their faces. Her voice shaking, Caroline said, "Please tell us what is going on."

The men presented badges from their jackets. "I am Agent Wills, and this is Agent Thompson. We will ask the questions. What are you doing here?"

Agent Thompson took their bags and emptied their contents onto a small table. He then opened their wallets and examined their driver's licenses.

Caroline explained who they were, how they came to be there, and the coincidence of finding the letter from Frank Lee. She talked about her disappointment with Sergeant Hope and that, having no confidence in the Police investigation, they had decided to see what they could find out.

Now regaining composure, Em said, "We've done nothing wrong, and if you know what is right, you will just let us go."

"Not that easy, I am afraid," said Thompson, who had now rifled through their belongings. "We need to find out more about you." Agent Thompson took their driver's licenses and left the apartment.

They were sitting there handcuffed to the chairs. Agent Wills said nothing. He was just half sitting, more leaning, on a window ledge, looking down at his shoes.

After a few minutes, Em said, "We have done nothing wrong. You should just let us go."

Agent Willis looked up. "You could be arrested for breaking and entering. You do understand that, right?" Not waiting for an answer, "You have no business here, and you have no idea what you are getting into." He stood up and said, "You two, just stay there. We'll be back soon." He went downstairs and stood outside the front door of the building, waiting.

Em said, "Where does he expect us to go with these handcuffs? Now what? I told you this was not a good idea."

Caroline interrupts, "We will be fine. We have done nothing wrong; you'll see."

Em rolled her eyes and nervously said, "Oh, if you call breaking and entering nothing, then we will be fine."

Minutes later, Thompson and Wills returned to the room and removed the handcuffs. Thompson pulled up a chair and sat facing them. With a slight nod from Wills and a severe look on his face, Thompson said,

"I don't think you know what you have stepped into here."

"Are you going to tell us?" Caroline asked.

The agents looked at each other, and both nodded their heads in agreement, "The man you are looking for, Frank Lee, has been under investigation as a possible war criminal. We have been watching him for some time. You may recall seeing a story on the news about a woman in Brooklyn who was arrested. She is an ex-Nazi prison guard who had been hiding in plain sight for years."

Caroline looked at Em with a shrug and recalled, "Only briefly yesterday on TV. We were more interested in the news about my dad being missing."

Thompson continued. "Well, the woman was arrested a couple of weeks ago, and she had information. Nothing of national interest but of great interest to the Simon Wiesenthal Organization; they are Nazi hunters."

Caroline interrupted, "I know who they are."

Thompson continued, "Since the war's end, the Wiesenthal Organization has searched for war criminals. They want justice for the millions of people slaughtered by the Nazis."

From his position by the door, Willis added, "The woman told us a story about people, money, and diamonds being smuggled from France to America towards the end of the war. She gave us information and confessed, hoping to avoid being sent back to Germany for trial. We found papers, documents, and diaries in her apartment. What we found led us to Frank Lee, who may not be who he says he is."

Agent Thompson added, "But we lost track of him. We are also looking for another woman. A Bette Caron. Ever heard of her?"

Em and Caroline looked at each other and shrugged.

"They were thought to be involved in a smuggling operation. We think this woman can lead us to others involved, other War Criminals."

Agent Wills took a seat and looked Caroline straight in the eye. "You must understand, we aren't the bad guys here. We only want to bring people to justice for the atrocities committed in the war. So, we get help wherever we can." He shifted on his chair and rubbed his fingers on his eyes as if pushing away a gritty feeling. He squeezed his nose beneath horned-rimmed, heavy-looking glasses. Looking at Caroline, "When you were going through your father's papers, was there anything else you found that you have not told the local police in Portland?" Em and Caroline were listening in total disbelief.

Em turned to Caroline and, with a furrowed brow, "This is getting weird. What on earth would Henry have to do with this?". Caroline was unaware she had been holding her breath as she processed what she was hearing. Her shoulders were slightly bent as she looked down. Conflicting emotions swirled within her. She straightened up and said, "There was a photo of a woman I had never seen and a message on the back thanking my dad for the help he had given her. Do you know who she is?"

"No"

"Do you still have the photo?"

"No." Caroline's stomach was nagging at her. "Last night, I was mugged outside the restaurant. My cash, checkbook, and credit cards were stolen, along with Frank Lee's note and the photo of the woman."

"Who knew you were in Boston looking for Frank Lee?"

Caroline picked up a pack of cigarettes from the table where all her stuff was spread out. She offered one to Emily.

"The only people who knew we were in Boston are my husband, Robert, and my uncle, Senator David Preston."

Willis asked, "David Preston, is your uncle?"

"Yes, he is my godfather. He is not really my uncle but a close family member." Feeling a little emboldened, Caroline continued, "And before you ask, there is no remote possibility that he could be involved. The only other person was the bartender at Myrtle's. So, if I were you, that is who I would be speaking to. He knows Frank Lee and probably knows where he is. Perhaps you can get it out of him."

Agent Wills stood up and walked to the window; Thompson joined him. Caroline and Em waited, blood drained from their faces and shaking a little, for whatever would happen next. Both agents turned as if looking out the window. With their backs to Caroline and Emily, they spoke so as not to be heard by the two women. After a minute of a whispered conversation, the men turned again to Caroline and Em.

Agent Thompson said, "OK, we are done here for now. I suggest you go home to Portland." He handed Caroline a card, "Take this, and if you find out who that woman is and she turns out to be Bette Caron, please call me, contact me straight away." Em and Caroline collected their belongings from the table.

Caroline turned to Agent Wills and said, "It was just an old photo, nothing more."

Willis added, "You have stepped into an FBI investigation. I'd be careful about how you handle things from now on. You should contact the police if there is anything else. In the meantime, let the police do their work, stay out of trouble, and go home to Portland."

Let's Get Out of Here

Badly shaken and relieved to be let go, Caroline and Emily left Frank Lee's apartment. They quickly walked to the corner and hailed a taxi. They didn't notice a green pickup parked on the corner, which followed them to the hotel. Arriving at Copley Plaza, Caroline asked the driver to wait. "We will be a few minutes; we just have to collect our bags."

The Bellman was at the front desk. Em handed him the receipt, and he went to get their bags. He warned them a winter storm was approaching. "According to the news, 6 to 10 inches of snow is expected by tomorrow morning."

"Do you have the train schedule?" Emily asked.

"There's a train at 12:30 and another, the last of the day, at 4 p.m."

Caroline took the schedule and gazed at it for a few seconds. Then, turning to Em, "We can be home by around seven tonight. But I still think we need to go and speak to the bartender one last time." And not waiting for an answer," We have nothing to lose. We're here anyway!"

Em stopped in her tracks. "Wait a minute, Caroline.

We have the taxi waiting and need to go. Let's get out of here."

Caroline replied, 'Yes! Yes, I know, but Em, I have to, and

I promise, the train after that. Please bear with me! It won't take long.

Em, shrugging her shoulder, "OK, if we must, we must."

They returned to the taxi and told the driver, "We have a slight change of plan. First, we want to stop at Myrtle's for a few minutes, just a few blocks."

At Myrtle's, the lunchtime crowd was beginning to fill the booths. A few people stood at the bar waiting for the barman's attention. A second person now served drinks and took orders for food. The place was noisier than before. Five minutes passed before Emily managed to get the barman's attention. He nodded in recognition, and Caroline said, "Can you give us a minute?"

"Hold on. I'll be right with you."

They waited, half watching the lunchtime news. Finally, the Barman asked, "What can I do for you? Did you find Frank?"

Caroline explained. "After we left here last night, I was mugged and," with a nod towards Em, "We were wondering if, by chance, you told anyone about our conversation?"

"Listen, I don't want any trouble, you hear!"

Em said, "We went to the yard where Frank Lee keeps his stuff. The owner, Mark, gave us the address of Frank's apartment. When we got there, it was a total mess. The FBI was watching the place and barged in on us. We were questioned and were lucky to get out of there without being arrested. Did you know they were looking for him as well?"

Now looking agitated, the barman said, "I don't know nothing about the FBI, and I don't want anything to do with the police. I serve drinks, listen to people's stories, and mind my business. I know nothing about muggings, FBI, or Franky besides what I told you. That's it. Now, if you don't mind, I have work." He turned and went to serve the next customer.

Em turned to Caroline, "Well, that's it. Let's go home."

"Yes, I guess." said Caroline, "Two days of following up leads and nothing but frustration."

As they left Myrtle's, it was beginning to snow again. The taxi was waiting for them. As they got in, Caroline told the cab driver, "Back to the Copley."

"Wait a minute," Em said, somewhat alarmed,

"I thought we were going for the train?"

"I know, but I can't do it. I need a bit more time. Please, Em, bear with me."

"Where are you going with this?" demanded Em. "We agreed!"

"Sorry, but I am staying till the storm has passed. I'll get the noon train tomorrow. I'm going back to the yard tomorrow to speak to Mark again. That's it. You can go home if you wish, I understand, but."

Emily interrupted. "No Way Jose! If you are staying, then so am I. Somebody will have to bail you out of jail next time you run afoul of the FBI."

Caroline reached across and squeezed Em's hand. "Thanks, what would I do without you?"

"Rot in prison, probably." Replied Em.

They paid for the taxi and entered the Copley Plaza lobby. Caroline went to the reception and asked if she could have a room for another night. She turned to Em. "I understand if you want to go home. I do, I really do Em!"

With some exasperation in her voice, Em replied. "No, I am here with you all the way." And pouting while shaking her head with a screwed-up face, "Even if you're not my favorite person right now." Caroline hugged her.

They collected their bags from the concierge and went to the room. No sooner had they started to unpack when the phone rang. Em picked it up.

A foreign-sounding voice said. "This is Frank Lee." Em almost jumped out of her skin. "I know you are looking for me." Em gestured at Caroline to come to the phone as she mouthed, "It's him."

Who? Caroline mouthed back.

"Him, Frank Lee!"

Caroline grabbed the phone from Em. "This is Caroline," she said as she caught her breath. "Where is my dad?"

The voice on the other end said, "You should stop looking for me. People will get hurt."

Caroline interrupted, "People, what people?

Why are you threatening me? What is this about?"

"Believe me. Your Dad would not want you to look for me. Let it be. Go back to Portland and allow a little time for things to sort themselves out."

Caroline held the phone slightly away from her head and waved to Emily to come and listen in. Both women stood next to each other, their hair touching, cheeks inches apart as they strained to hear what Frank Lee said.

"Where is my dad? Where is he?" She demanded.

"I don't know where he is. He was supposed to meet me but didn't show up."

Caroline demanded, "You must meet me. I need to talk with you."

"No, I do not have to do anything." The accented voice replied in a deliberate tone.

Now, almost climbing down the phone, Caroline said, "There is no way I am going to let this be. I don't know anything about you, but I will find out. My first stop will be with the police." Em looked at Caroline and moved her hands up and down, mouthing "S-L-O-W." Caroline nodded in agreement and turned her attention back to Frank Lee.

"I have already spoken to the FBI. They were at your apartment. We were there looking for you. The door was not locked. We went in, and then they burst in on us.

"I know."

"How do you know? You had better start telling me what is going on! Why are they looking for you?"

Frank Lee said, "The police will only make things worse. People will be hurt, and you do not want that. You have a family, children, and a business. You don't want to drag your family down in the mud. If you continue, you will endanger people's lives."

Caroline's face was tight as she tried to control her

anger. Trying to maintain her composure, she took a deep breath as mild panic washed over her. A stream of questions raced through her mind.

Despite Em's encouragement to slow down, she could not stop. "What, for God's sake, do you mean, drag my family down into the mud? Why are you calling me if you won't answer my questions? "Caroline followed up with a string of questions asked one after the other, spitting them out like bullets from a machine gun.

"Stop trying to find me. I will find you when the time is right, and I need your help. Will you help me? Henry said he would help me?"

"My Dad said he would help you?"

"I can't talk now. You must return to Portland, and I will contact you when the time is right."

The phone clicked, and looking at Em, "He hung up." Caroline dropped the phone on the bed and went to the window.

Pulling the drapes to one side, she looked out as if expecting to see somebody standing on the twenty-fifth floor. She turned and rushed out the door, followed by Em, both wearing only their socks and with Emily on her heels, Caroline quickly reached the elevator and punched the button. Em pushed the button again as if a second push would make it come faster. Caroline was impatient and pressed it again, saying, "Come on, come on."

It seemed like an eternity as the little lights above the door lit up as the elevator passed through the floors below. Finally, it arrived. They got in, pushed the button for the Lobby, waited, and pushed it again before the doors closed. The elevator arrived at the lobby with a ding. They did not give the elevator door time to open fully. They pushed past the half-open door and rushed to the Concierge. Caroline asked, "Has someone, a man with an accent, been looking for me?"

Taken by surprise, the concierge looked up from the note he was writing on a pad in front of him. "What's your name and room number?" He paused for a second and looked at a list on his desk. "Yes," pointing to the house phone on a desk, "over there a few minutes ago." But the phone was back in its cradle, and nobody was there. He added, "Well, he was there a few minutes ago."

Caroline's heart was pounding, and her face was red. Em, wide-eyed, turned on her heels and quickly walked to the front entrance, followed by Caroline. The sidewalk was wet from the heavy winter snow falling in large flakes. Their feet got soaked without coats and only their socks for warmth; they held their arms around themselves to keep out the cold. A couple, arm in arm with heads down, brushed past them and into the hotel. A man with his collar turned up entered a taxi in front of the hotel. A small green pickup truck on the other side of the street pulled away from the curb. A light went on in Caroline's head as she recalled the conversation about Frank Lee and his hot dog wagon. She stepped forward, arms in the air as if hailing a cab, and called, "Wait, stop!" But they were just a minute too late. The small green pickup turned the corner and was gone.

She turned to Emily. "Shit, that was him in the green truck. He's gone." They stood in the street, snow falling as they stared into the distance. Em put her arm around Caroline's waist and guided her, "Come on, let's go back inside. It's cold out here. We'll find him, don't worry."

They returned to their room, sat on opposite beds, and silently removed their wet socks. Caroline was staring at the phone on the bedside table, willing it to ring again and praying he had a change of heart.

She lay on the bed, head on the pillow, arms at her side, staring up. She was transfixed as she mentally reviewed what had happened. Moments later, Caroline sat bolt upright. "He is looking for help. He said so. I wonder what exactly he needs, and why did Dad offer to help him?".

Em added, "If Henry did offer to help him, why not

just meet with you and tell you what is happening?"

Caroline replied, "We can't be sure at this point. His behavior doesn't lead me to trust what he says, but it seems he cares about what happens. That is my hope. Which means he will contact me again. He doesn't want us talking to the police, and he knows they are looking for him. That's it. We know the FBI is looking for him. I think he will contact me again and hopefully help me find out what happened to Dad. Sooner rather than later, I hope."

"So," Em said, "does that mean we should check out again and go home?"

Caroline got up from the bed. "I'm exhausted after all the chasing around. How about you?"

"Let's go home. It's been a tough day."

"Yes," said Caroline, "but I am not giving up, not now. There is no turning back. Somehow, I will get to the bottom of this and find out what happened to my dad and his involvement with Frank Lee."

So, there it is. A hunch, a feeling in your stomach that beckons you. It calls you, and you have no option but to follow your instincts. Resisting is impossible, no matter how often people tell you to let it go. Caroline marches to the beat of her own drum, and she will find a way or make a way. Turning back is not an option for her.

Return To Portland

They were back in Portland by 7 pm. Emily and Caroline walked together to the parking lot.

"Em, I'm unsure what I would have done without you. Hopefully, I'll find Robert sober enough to explain what has happened."

"You know he will be furious that you did not tell him you were mugged. I can see it now."

"Yes, but once I explain everything, he will understand it was for the best. I am fine, and he didn't have to imagine me standing in the cold with blood dripping down my face, thinking all kinds of terrible things."

"So, what happens now?" "How do you mean?"

"Well, with Frank Lee and Canada? Are you still planning to go?"

"I don't know about Canada.

David said he wanted to come with me just in case."

"In case of what?"

"I am not sure. Something has been nagging at me. Uncle David said I should be careful about turning over stones when we spoke on the phone. It sounded strange, but he's coming to lunch this weekend anyway. Perhaps I'll find out more. Tell you what, you should also come since you have a clearer head than me."

"I have a client in town I need to spend some time with. I will call you tomorrow and confirm. Hopefully, I'll see you then. Take care." They hugged again and made their way to their respective cars.

A man standing in the shadows, wearing a heavy winter coat and an imitation fur hat, about six-foot-tall, with dark-rimmed glasses, was watching them. Agent Wills had followed the two women onto the train. He found his way out of the concourse and to the car rental agency, where he picked up a car and drove to a local hotel. The following day, he would meet with Sergeant Hope to share thoughts and ideas about what would come next.

* * *

Caroline arrived home, pulled into her driveway, and parked in front of the middle garage. The house looked welcoming, as always. She exited the car and got her overnight bag from the back seat. The lights were on in all the windows, and as she approached the door, she could see the blue light of the TV flashing. She was glad to be home.

She entered the foyer, kicked off her boots, dropped her bag on the floor, and went to the family room, calling,

"Robert, Mike, Ricky, Melissa, I'm home." She found her three children watching Happy Days on the TV. Mike and Ricky spread out across the two sofas, and Melissa, the youngest, was in the easy chair, her back on one armrest and her legs casually hanging over the other.

As Caroline walked into the room, all three sat up. Mike picked up the TV remote and turned the sound down. Caroline took her coat off and playfully threw it over Melissa's head. "Hey, what's going on here?" She was smiling and pleased to be home, finding her kids tucked up together and watching TV. "Where's Dad?"

There was a brief silence as her children looked at each other. Mike said, "Upstairs in bed," and indifferently, "passed out probably."

She turned immediately and hurried upstairs to the bedroom. Opening the door, "Robert," she called as she entered the room. "Robert, wake up." She saw his head in a pool of vomit as she approached the bed and repeated his name, "Robert, wake up." But he did not respond. His breathing was shallow, his face pale blue. She shook him and slid her arm under his neck, but there was no change. She grabbed tissues from the bedside table and wiped vomit from around his nose and mouth. She turned Robert on his side and put a pillow under his head. Picking up the phone from the bedside table, she called 911. "My husband is drunk, passed out, and I can't wake him up. I need an ambulance. Quickly, please help me."

She patiently answered the operator's questions and was told to keep him warm, on his side, and that an ambulance would be there very soon. She put the phone down and continued to try to wake Robert. He began to rouse. He was coughing and spluttering as he slowly came out of his stupor.

Caroline helped him to sit up. "How could you do this, to be so stupid? What on earth is the matter with you?" Her emotions were all over the place. In seconds, she went from being scared to angry to concerned, terrified, and back to angry again. Then, trying to get the proper response, "Don't worry, we will take care of you. An ambulance is on the way. I thought you were dead. Robert, this is the last time. We can't do this again."

Robert was taken to Portland Medical Center. Caroline followed with Mike, Ricky, and Melissa and waited until they were sure he would be OK. The following day, Robert was transferred to a rehab center to see if he could shake the grip alcohol had over him.

Sunday Lunch

David Preston pulled into the driveway and parked on one side of the garage. He set the brake on the 1972 Ford Bronco, a first-generation four-wheel drive. It had an outdoor look tempered by the dark red color and chrome trim. It made more of a city statement than the rugged outdoors. Whenever she saw him with the car, Emily Whitt teased him, asking when he would go 'rock jumping' in it. But it suited David and was safer in the snow than the big lumbering Cadillac he used in the summer. Stepping from the Bronco onto a somewhat snowy driveway, David walked to the porch of Caroline's house. He stamped his feet to shed the snow, walked up the three steps, and pushed the bell button. He knocked on the door, opened it, stepped into the hallway, and called, "Caroline, hello. Anyone home?"

Caroline and Em were in the kitchen. With a glass of wine in her hand, Em watched as Caroline placed some cheese and crackers on a board. She called out to David, "We're in here, in the kitchen," Caroline put the last crackers on the board and walked down the hallway to meet David halfway. At the same time, Melissa ran from the living room.

David crouched down, and she threw herself into his arms, giving him a big hug." Are you going to help us find Pops? We don't know where he is?"

"We are trying, sweetie. I'm sure we will find him soon."

"Dad is in the hospital again." Said with a down-turned pursed lip, "He is going to be there till…sometime."

"I know. Your dad will get better soon, I'm sure of it."

Caroline put her arm around Melissa's shoulder. "Set the table so we can all have a nice lunch." Melissa turned and wandered off, muttering about why Mike or Ricky couldn't do it.

Caroline hugged David, turned, and invited him to the kitchen. "Any news?" he asked.

Over her shoulder, "Nothing new since we last spoke." As they entered the kitchen, Emily greeted David with a hug.

A cloud hung over them during their simple lunch: Henry's absence, understandably the main topic of conversation. After the meal, Mike, Ricky, and Melissa helped clear the table. They took the dishes to the kitchen, and then the two boys wandered off to watch the game on TV. It was Superbowl Sunday, and the Miami Dolphins were against the Minnesota Vikings.

David, Emily, and Caroline were sitting at the dining table as Caroline came to her real agenda. "David, since we talked on the phone the other day, what you said about 'not turning over stones' has been ringing in my ears. What did you mean?"

David looked down at the coffee before him, picked up a spoon, and stirred as he searched his mind for the correct answer. Pushing his lips together as if trying to hold something back, he looked up at Caroline. He was having trouble finding the right words.

"OK, look, the only thing I can tell you is this guy, Frank, was somebody your dad helped 'back in the day.'"

Emily interrupted. "How far back in the day?"

"Well, I have not heard his name for years, and honestly," looking at Caroline, "I was a bit taken aback when you started talking about him. Hearing his name like that, out of the blue, took me by surprise.

I shouldn't have responded that way."

"And?" Asked Caroline.

"He was, is, a Frenchman. We err, your dad, helped him get to America from England when we ran transport ops in Europe during the war."

Caroline interrupted. "Why would Dad do that?"

"It feels like you're interrogating me," David protested. "Honestly, Caroline, I don't know. That's all I can tell you. I have not heard from him, and the only reason I said not to turn over stones was that, well, your dad 'may' have taken some money from him for the transport."

Ignoring his protest about being interrogated, Em asked, "So, that's the problem? Is it possible that Frank Lee is blackmailing Henry?"

David replied, "Well, no, not really. I don't know. It could be. It would have been a problem back then. He would have had the military to answer to. Now I am not sure." Caroline and Em listened patiently, silently waiting for David to continue.

David said, "This is all in the past, and we should just let it rest. You can be assured he, Frank Lee, if that's what he still calls himself, has nothing to do with your dad disappearing."

With her voice raised, Caroline asked, "How can you be so certain?" Her face turned red as her emotions got the better of her.

Em interrupted and tried to calm things down. "Well, if Henry would prefer to keep this private, which he must have, perhaps we should just leave it and let the police do their work."

"Yes, that makes sense," David eagerly agreed.

"If Henry wanted to keep this Frank thing private, we should respect his wishes."

Caroline regained her composure, "Hold on. You just said if that is what he still calls himself. Why should he call himself anything different?"

David thought for a minute. "He changed his name to become American. When your dad knew him, he was Francois Leblanc, a Frenchman. Your dad helped him with papers after he got to America. But this is all so far in the past. What's done is done." Caroline nodded slightly at Em and then turned back to David. "How will we keep this private if the FBI is after him now?"

David's face turned white. He looked like a deer caught in the headlights. "What on earth are you talking about? The FBI?"

Ignoring the question, Caroline continued, "And what is he hiding from them?"

David shifted in his chair. He put his coffee cup back on the table, buying precious seconds to organize his thoughts, desperate to exit this conversation. The room was silent for a few seconds. Caroline waited, then looked at David and added,

"What could Frank Lee mean when telling me to let

things go because people could get hurt?"

David was alarmed again. "You have spoken to Frank Lee? When? How did you find him?"

Caroline again ignored David's question. "You and my dad have known each other all your lives. What's going on? If you want me to understand, you must explain what stones I should not be turning over?"

David gathered his thoughts, "I am not saying anything more until you tell me what happened in Boston."

They then told him the whole story. They talked about the bar, the yard with the hot dog guys, finding the apartment, the FBI, the call to the hotel, and the mugging, which, despite Em disagreeing, Caroline said, "I am certain it was not a mugging. "They must have been after my evidence," she insisted.

David Preston sat in silence and listened, weighing his options. Then, quite casually, he said, "Well, if that is the case, then we best hope Frank Lee finds you before the FBI finds him!"

"Why?" Caroline and Em asked in unison and then looked at each other with the very slightest of smirks.

David quickly responded, "If you can talk to him, maybe he needs some help, perhaps money. My guess is he does not want the FBI to find him. Maybe we should help him to keep your dad out of this."

"We?" Caroline asked.

David said, "Well, yes, of course. Caroline, I have known you since the day you were born. Of course, I want to help you."

"I am thinking of going to Canada to follow the other lead. You know, the article I found on Dad's desk. Maybe even find out more about Frank Lee. Also, if he contacts me again, he may be able to help me find the woman in the photo. The one I told you about was probably thrown away by the person who mugged me." She may know something more.

"I'll come with you to Canada." David insisted. "And you must let me know if Frank contacts you again. You don't know him, and he may be dangerous. Promise you'll tell me, and we can ensure you are not alone if you meet him."

Caroline hesitated. She decided not to push any further. Although she had questions about why David thought Frank Lee would be a danger to her, she agreed but was not convincing to either Em or David.

David pushed his chair away from the table and said, "I must get going. I have to prepare for meetings with some environmental people tomorrow and then go to Washington on Tuesday. Please keep me updated, and Caroline, don't do anything without telling me first." She nodded, and they hugged. "Thanks for lunch, and please keep me informed, Okay?" Caroline nodded, and both Em and Caroline walked David to the door. He hollered goodbye to the Kids as he put on his boots and coat. Caroline and Em watched him get in the Bronco and drive away.

* * *

David Preston pulled into the first gas station and stopped by a public phone. He picked up the handset, put a dime in the slot, and dialed a number he had committed to memory. "It's me; meet me in the bar at the Copley Plaza at nine this evening. There is someone I want you to find and send him on a very long vacation, urgently."

He hung up the phone, returned to the Bronco, and drove to Boston.

Mist of Time Rehab

Robert, now stable and on a saline drip to rehydrate him, was transferred from the hospital to a rehab center in New Hampshire. The clinic, from the outside, appeared to be a private home. Set in rolling hills with views of the White Mountains, the facility provided medical care, individual therapy, group meetings, and a supportive environment. It was a secluded place where those who could afford the fees could work on getting their lives back.

The treatment was total abstinence. Once the person had completed the initial phase, which could take two to five days, it was time to start the therapy. Patients were usually able to check out within four to six weeks.

While there, they must attend group discussions and one-to-one counseling. The clinic used drugs to help with convulsions, seizures, hallucinations, depression, confusion, nausea, vomiting, shakes, and tremors. Typically, patients have used alcohol to avoid deep-seated problems and associated emotional pain, albeit outside their immediate consciousness.

Cognitive behavior therapy, counseling, and psychotherapy are combined to help patients understand their problems and the underlying causes.

Robert went through the "drying out" agony for three days. For most of the time, he was curled up in bed at the clinic, like an unborn baby in the fetal position. Having done it before, he was mentally ready for the struggle ahead of him. This third attempt, he was determined, would be his last. Mentally, he was ready.

In moments of clarity in bed, he would give himself pep talks: "If I can get through this now, there is a chance that Caroline will not finally kick me out. I couldn't blame her if she did. It's my fault. I should have been there for her, and with Henry missing, things are not any easier."

Between being awake and conscious and medically induced sleeping, there was a middle ground when he was neither fully awake nor fully asleep. During such periods, he was plagued by demons and had tortured dreams.

"They will get me, spiders crawling all over me, dirt in my mouth. It's on my head, hands, all over me, no. Oh no, who is screaming? I can help them. What is banging? What is that light, and where? There, jump, run. I am so cold, shivering. Please let me die. I love them." He was relieved from this torture when in a deep, drug-induced sleep.

"Time to wake up, Robert." Gentle hands slid beneath his shoulders, and a calm voice gently called his name.

" Robert, wake up."

He resisted. "No, the spiders are getting me. Stop hurting me. Everything is hurting me." And aloud to himself, his legs trying to move independently of any conscious desire to move and pleading to an unseen power, "Help me get away. I must go now."

"Robert, Wake Up." He slowly opened his eyes to see a nurse in medical scrubs with her arm under his shoulder. She was saying something, but Robert could not understand. His head hurt, and his mouth was drier than sawdust. She gently raised his weary body from the bed and held a glass of orange juice to his lips. She was talking to him, but his ears rang, and he could not understand what she was saying. Then he was overtaken by darkness. He cycled between being awake and asleep. The hallucinations went on for three days and nights.

During this challenging time, Robert confronted glimpses of his past as a child and then as an adult at college. He relived the early days with Caroline, ready to take on the world and create a future: the past, present, and an imagined, tormented future world all in one.

Coming in and out of consciousness, Robert no longer knew what was real. Sometimes, with the dreams and delirium abating, he gained enough awareness to see the kind face of a nurse helping him swallow pills or gently bathe his face and neck with a cool cloth.

"It will be OK, Robert, you will see. Soon, you will feel better." He would take a sip of juice, swallow the pills, and drift back to another world that was scary, strange, and yet somehow familiar.

On the morning of the fourth day, Robert awoke feeling exhausted. The pains and chills had evaporated. He lay in bed and began to take stock. Looking around, he could see outside the sun was shining, and across a snow-covered lawn, a tennis court, now closed for winter. There were park benches and a gazebo with one person in the cold, bundled up in a downy jacket. Robert took in the room. Pictures hung on the walls. On one, a tranquil beach scene, and on another, a forest with light streaming through the trees. The third wall had somebody skiing down a mountain in deep snow with the words, find a Way or Make a Way, and another with a flock of birds on a seashore with the caption: We Are All in This Together!

The door opened, and Nurse Bryant came into the room. "Good morning, Robert."

Robert recognized her. "Is it a good morning? I hope so." He had met her when he was signed in, and all the paperwork was complete. He could now see her name tag and added, "Thanks, Jackie, thanks for taking care of me. How bad was it?"

Nurse Bryant was a petite woman with a big smile. Trim and a bit starchy, she was in her mid-forties. She had been with Robert most of the time he went through the agonizing torment of detoxification.

"You'll be fine now. I know it. This was rough for you. If you don't want to ever go through that agony again, you <u>will</u> stay here for the next four weeks and do the therapy."

Robert had previously agreed to this, as he had before, but never followed through. This time, the stakes were higher.

"Time to take a shower and a shave. There are clean clothes in the bathroom." She helped him get out of bed. He was wearing a hospital gown tied up at the back. At first, he was unsteady but could get to the bathroom with Nurse Bryant's help.

"I will be back in half an hour, and we can get you some breakfast."

"Ugh," Robert growled, "not sure I can face anything."

Once he was in the bathroom with the water running, she left him to get on with it. Robert looked in the mirror and noticed his beard and the dark shadows around his eyes. His hair was messy, and he told himself, "Good grief, you look bad, and I feel like shit."

Over the next few days, Robert bounced back. In the next few weeks, he attended the group sessions and the one-to-one counseling with the psychiatrist, Dr. Michael. The therapists took him through a series of regressions—slowly taking him back to his childhood. The therapy peeled back the layers of what he had buried deep inside his mind. He worked through the tears and allowed a shining light into the darkness. When he broke down and cried, Robert was held and comforted, enabling him to complete the picture that had been a blur throughout his life.

The FBI Is Watching

Agent Willis threw his hat, gloves, and coat onto an empty chair as he entered the Portland Police conference room. The room was light and airy, with windows on Portland's Middle Street. Sergeant Hope, Lieutenant Watts, and Captain Mathews were in the room waiting for him. What had started as a missing person report now involved the upper levels of police management and the FBI.

Agent Willis opened the discussion. "Since the war's end in Europe, we have been working with the Simon Wiesenthal Organization, helping them bring war criminals to justice. A few weeks ago, we caught Hermine Braunstein. She was a Nazi prison guard at Ravensbruck and Majdanek concentration camps. She is an awful, wicked person. She was known to have whipped people to death and, grabbing them by the hair, threw women and children onto trucks before being taken to their deaths in the gas chambers. She hanged young female prisoners and stomped old women to death with her jackboots."

The three officers had manila folders opened before them and turned pages as Agent Willis described the nastiness and depths of the guard's depravity. Captain Mathews interrupted.

"My God! I have met some depraved people, but this woman is truly evil."

Agent Willis nodded in agreement and continued, "She'd been living in Brooklyn for many years. She was hiding in plain sight, as it were. Thanks to the Wiesenthal Organization's work, we tracked her down. She was arrested a couple of weeks ago. We let the news media know we had her a few days ago. When we've finished questioning her, she'll be sent to Germany to stand trial. In the meantime, she has provided us with information. She hopes cooperating will help her get a reduced penalty. We can't be sure what lies she is spinning, so we have kept her on a promise, but it will not happen. She will probably hang.

Sergeant Hope said, "That sounds too kind! But what has she told you about Frank Lee?"

"It's a bit vague," Agent Willis continued. She told us she ran into him in Boston a few years ago. Frank Lee is a street vendor who works near Myrtles Bar. He sells hot dogs near the Boston Public Library, including during winter if it is not too cold. He is known as Frenchy and has been in the U.S.A. since the Second World War.

Captain Mathews, a heavy-set man with a dark

mustache, commented, "The kind of work that deals in cash and helps him to stay under the radar." Willis nodded in agreement.

Lieutenant Watts asked,

"Anything more about their connection in Paris?"

Agent Willis replied, "Not much, according to Braunstein; she knew him from their time there after the German invasion. She told us that Frank Lee was an officer involved in the round-up of Jews.

Those who did not resist were sent to the holding camps north of Paris. Those who did, sometimes entire families, were summarily shot in front of their neighbors. The French Militia cooperated with the Gestapo in the round-up. In addition to the Jews, they seized members of the resistance and other minorities. Drancy, the largest camp, was in the northeast of Paris and the first stop before being sent to Auschwitz, Dachau, or Buchenwald concentration Camp. We have not found anything that corroborates what she told us about how she knew Frank Lee."

"And the connection to Henry Stern?" asked Lieutenant Watts.

Willis turned the page in his folder, "According to Hermine Braunstein, Frank Lee has a connection to Henry Stern's past. We do not have a way to corroborate that. Either she could not or would not tell us what that connection was.

It may be a lie, but she told us about people trying to escape France, which is not a crime. Given the Gestapo, I would also want to get away. Anyway, she seemed to think a lot of money, maybe diamonds, was involved. She insists Lee is German. I guess we will find out soon enough."

Sergeant Hope added, "He is a slippery S.O.B. Any idea how he knew you were looking for him?"

Lieutenant Watts said, "The community where he hangs out is close-knit, honor among thieves and all that. If we poke around and ask questions, people get wind of it and disappear."

Agent Willis turned the page on his folder, "There is another woman involved, Bette Caron. We think she was a collaborator and an analyst. But there is no real evidence, just what we know from other cases and notes in the papers we got from Braunstein's apartment," and addressing all three officers, "Copies are also in your folders, but as I said, I think Braunstein is holding some things back, for now. She probably wants to use whatever else she has as leverage for reduced sentencing. We will play along until we don't!"

Agent Willis closed the folder he had in front of him and continued. "The last pages in your folders are copies of documents and photos we got from her."

"Do you have any more insight on Henry Stern?"

asked Lieutenant Watts as he got up and went to get more coffee.

Willis replied, "Well, probably no more than what you already have. He is an American and served his country in the war. After the war, he appears to have led an honest life. He developed Stern Trucking and Shipping, and since finding his daughter at Lee's apartment, we now know he is close friends with Senator Preston of Maine. They play bridge at the local club together, but not recently".

Sergeant Hope commented with a slight grin, "Frankly, I don't get it." By the look on the faces of the senior officers in the room, they did not appreciate the joke.

Now more seriously, Sergeant Hope said. "After you called yesterday, we got a wiretap order. Previously, we didn't have cause. Now, with the connection to war crimes, the judge was convinced. We'll let you know if we get anything".

Captain Mathews said, "If Sterns's daughter had not gone to find Frank Lee, we wouldn't have known about his connection. We have been looking for Stern, but you never know with missing people reports. Maybe he disappeared himself. Maybe somebody else, for whatever reason, took him. Somebody in his position can be at risk of being held for ransom, so we tread carefully. At this point, we do not know what Frank Lee's connection is to Henry Stern. We know that Stern and Lee have disappeared, and they may be together, and maybe not."

Sergeant Hope responded, "Until yesterday, when you found her at Lee's apartment, we did think it possible that Caroline knew where Stern was, but since she went looking for Frank Lee, I don't think that theory holds water."

Captain Mathews looked at Sergeant Hope and said, "Too bad you missed those notes his daughter found. But, I guess, even if you had seen them, they wouldn't have meant anything to you, probably not have made a difference anyway."

Looking a little sheepish, Seargent Hope added, "We are continuing to keep an eye on her, but honestly, I think any chance of her leading us to Henry Stern is unlikely. I don't think she knows his whereabouts. If she does, she deserves an Oscar!" Agent Willis continued the discussion, "I followed her from Boston back here to Portland last night, and she went straight home. Emily Whitt was with her, but I doubt she knows anything that can help."

Sergeant Hope added, "After Mrs. Hall got home, her husband, Robert, was taken to the hospital by ambulance."

"How's that?" Willis asked with a furrowed brow.

"Well," Sgt Hope explained, "The guy has a problem

with alcohol. He's been in and out of rehab and can't seem to kick a period habit.

Agent Willis continued, "OK, so he is out of the picture for now at least, and we know where to find him if needed. Also, when we interviewed Mrs. Hall at Lee's apartment, she told us about coming to Boston and Myrtles Bar looking for Lee—some story about being mugged. I checked with the locals, and at least that part seems true. The rest is in the file for you to read."

Captain Mathews said, "So, even though we would have preferred that she not go snooping for Lee, she has now made a connection between him and Henry Stern." The officers in the room nodded in agreement as Captain Mathews continued. "Well, if that's it for now, I have another meeting." Looking at Sergeant Hope, "Please keep us informed of anything else. Stern is a prominent person in the community, not to mention anything about Senator Preston. We do not want this to become a public relations issue."

Agent Willis stood up, shook the captain's hand, and said, "Thanks for the cooperation. While Lee has slipped from sight, we will find him. We need to find out if there is a connection between Braunstein, Lee, and Stern. I doubt it somehow, but you never know!" then, quoting Sir Walter

Scott, he said, "Oh, what a tangled web we weave when first we practice to deceive."

Henry's Demise

Henry Stern was a large man with a full, well-trimmed beard, a little overweight, a bit too much overweight. His doctor would remind him of his heart condition and tell him to lose weight, and Henry insisted he felt fine.

He was calm, pleasant, and generally had a good nature. He could be stubborn and sometimes had a volcanic temper that could erupt when sufficiently antagonized. The bright side of his stubborn nature was that he could be incredibly and uncompromisingly loyal to his friends. His relationships, the real ones, were established slowly and lasted a lifetime.

On the afternoon before his disappearance, Henry was at home sitting at his desk in the 'Lions Den.' He was preparing for a meeting with banks and investors as he considered taking Stern Trucking and Shipping public. It was Monday, Jan 7th, and Henry had decided to work from home to avoid interruptions at the office. The following morning, he was to have breakfast with his daughter, Caroline. He wanted her input on some ideas and to assure her of her role as she had now returned to work at ST&S.

The phone rang, and he answered. "I said I did not want to be disturbed." The voice on the other end was from the past. It was a person he knew and had recently emerged, much to his chagrin.

His mind raced as he was, even then, calculating how to get rid of this person permanently.

Memories he buried long ago were flooding his mind.

"Henry," Frank Lee said. "We must meet soon. I need your help."

"Are you out of your fucking mind? I told you in Boston never to contact me again. I gave you money. You were supposed to disappear!"

"I know, but this is an emergency, and you could be in danger."

Henry exploded down the phone, "What the fuck are you talking about?"

Lee continued, "When we met, I thought I was being followed, and I was being careful. I am sure I am in danger after all these years, and I know they are looking for me. Did you see the news about that bitch, Hermine Braunstein? They arrested her in Brooklyn two weeks ago. She is a nasty person without any morals. I know her reputation as a guard. I think she will have given them information that compromises me. She knows me and may have blown the whistle on me."

Henry calmed down, but just a little. "I read she was a prison guard in a concentration camp. But how does that affect me? She doesn't know me from Adam!"

"But she knows me, and I'm sure they are coming for me soon. And, well, I will not have a choice other than to tell them what I know."

Henry understood his involvement would be all over the news. The message was loud and clear. He was being blackmailed. If he refused, Frank Lee would destroy him. His business, family, and everything he had worked for. "You must help me," Lee said.

Henry pulled himself together, "Listen, we can't talk on the phone. I will meet you."

Lee interrupted, "Will you, Henry, will you? I have no other way to get out of the country and can't go back after all these years. You are my only hope."

Henry's mind was racing with thoughts of the past and future colliding. He was constructing images of different possible outcomes.

"Drive to Canada, go to Quebec, and stay at the Borderline Inn. You will be safe and among friends. I'll make the arrangements for you. It's about a six-hour drive from Boston, and you must leave immediately. It's four thirty now, so you should arrive before 11 tonight. I will be there tomorrow morning; I must change some meetings. But don't worry. I'll help you get away on one of our container ships. One is leaving in a few days for South America."

Frank Lee was resigned to his fate, "Yes, Okay, but."

Henry was getting impatient. "No buts! Do as I tell you and do it straight away. You must go to the airport and get a Hertz rental. I will make the reservation in your name. Tell them Harold Lemoine made the reservation." He carefully spelled it out. L-E-M-O-I-N-E. "Just give them your name and driving license. If they want to confirm the address of the credit card, tell them it is Rue Alfred 1731 Quebec. That's all the information they will need. Leave your vehicle in the long-term car park, go to arrivals, and take the shuttle bus to the rental office. Do you understand?"

"Yes, I understand."

"I hope so. Make sure no one follows you. Got it?" Yes, I got it. Frank Lee said.

Henry added, "Once you park and before you get on the shuttle if you suspect anyone has their eyes on you, take steps to ensure you are clean."

"Okay, I can do that. But I don't have very much money."

Henry took a deep breath, feeling angry again, but controlled the urge and said, "I will bring some cash to help you. It is your only chance. You have an American Passport and will easily cross the border. Few, if any, questions are ever asked. But if asked about your business in Canada, say you are there for a vacation with family. If they ask where you are staying, tell them you are going to the Borderline Hotel in Quebec City."

Frank Lee responded, "I will do as you say."

Henry had now calmed down a little. "Good, I'll call the hotel, and I am warning you, don't fucking call me here again." He hung up the phone, stared at it for a minute, picked it up again, called Hertz at the Airport, and made the car reservation. He hung up again and then dialed the Borderline Hotel in Quebec.

"A woman picked up the phone, and with a French accent, Borderline Hotel, can I help you."

"Claire, It's Henry."

"There you are! Are you coming to see me?"

"I am, but there's a potential problem, and you have to know about it," Henry explained the situation to Claire, who was dumbstruck.

"Why here? I hate that man; he will recognize me. He knows who I am. Henry, there has to be another way?"

"I wouldn't do this if I didn't have to. I have to get Lee away from me. He must not be seen and cannot get caught. Just stay out of his way. Make an excuse and get your help to welcome him."

"But Christy isn't not working tonight!"

"Okay, just leave an envelope with his key at reception. I know you do this for late arrivals sometimes. You leave the Inn, book into the Frontenac, and wait for me. I will be there tonight and meet up with him when he arrives; I will be there before him. I know you understand how important this is, Claire. If they find him, they'll find you. God knows what will happen to us all. I will do whatever it takes. You understand, right?"

"Yes, Henry, I trust you."

"Don't be scared. I want you to be ready. Remember the plan we made just in case something like this happened."

Claire responded, "Yes, will it come to that?"

"I don't think so, I hope not, but pack a bag and get what cash you can. I will bring more. Bring the papers I left for you. I had hoped we would never have to use them. And we may not need to. But be ready to run, just in case. I don't want you getting caught up in any of this. I will arrange your travel back to Europe with a different name. I will look after you. I love you, don't worry."

Henry hung up, thought for a few minutes, and then called the Copley Plaza in Boston. He booked a room for two nights in his name, saying he would be a late arrival. He thought he might not make it to Boston. If Caroline called when he did not show up for breakfast and did not get to call her before she read the note he planned to leave on the kitchen counter, the hotel would say he had a two-day reservation.

Depending on how it worked out, he would have time to get to Boston from Quebec and arrive early or call tonight and let them know he would be there late because of travel delays. In any case, he would have to call Caroline in the morning, and if all was well, it would be from Boston, or it would appear that he was in Boston. He did not want anyone to know he was in Quebec.

His chest had begun to hurt. He opened his desk drawer and took out a small bottle of pills. He swallowed two without water, picked up his jacket from the chair next to the desk, put it on, and put the rest of the pills in the jacket pocket.

He went to the kitchen, drank water, and went upstairs to his bedroom. Kneeling beside the bed, he pulled back the rug and exposed the safe under the bed. The safe opened with three turns to the left, two to the right, one more left, and another turn to the right. Inside were neatly banded stacks of twenties, fifties, one hundred dollar bills, and a small revolver, German and unregistered. His hands wrapped around the stock as images slowly came to mind, memories he chased away.

He put the gun in his bag with a box of shells and five thousand dollars of bundled notes. He grabbed a change of clothes from the neatly arranged shirts, jackets, and pants from his dressing room and stuffed them in the bag. It was just after 4 pm. Time was pressing, and he needed to be on his way if he was to arrive in good time to carry out his plan. According to his calculation, the drive would take five hours. He figured he would arrive in time if the predicted weather held up. If all went well, and without any sleep, he could return to Boston and call Caroline from the hotel in the morning.

He left a note in the kitchen for her. They often found that meeting in the morning at home ensured privacy and minimal interruptions. They had arranged to have breakfast together at 8 a.m.

He wrote: Caroline, I had to leave for Boston tonight and meet some folks early in the morning. I Don't want you to worry, and I will call you before the meeting.

All good, love Dad.

Henry got in his Jeep and drove out of the driveway,

over the Casco Bay bridge separating South Portland from the downtown, onto Commercial Street, and then 95, heading North to Waterville. He then took route 201 towards Quebec City.

He figured it would be Okay if the snow did not worsen. It had been a warm late December; the usual January thaw came early, and the weather had become unpredictable.

Heading further North, visibility became poor as he wound his way on Route 201, through forests, lakes, and the occasional small towns with a gas station, convenience store, and perhaps a diner. The further North he went, the more deserted it became. There was more snow than anticipated, and he had to slow down a little, but he figured he had plenty of time. And time for him to figure out if he would use the money or the gun. He decided to wait and see how things unfolded in Quebec.

It had been a long time since this type of emergency threatened him. Life had become legitimate, and now everything he worked for could be in jeopardy. He would not let that happen; it was not in his nature. Henry Stern could be ruthless, no matter who else got hurt. He was a man who could always figure out what he wanted and how to get it, regardless.

The weather deteriorated, made worse by the occasional logging trucks and fuel tankers that hurtled towards him, headlights piercing the snowy darkness. The lights of the oncoming vehicles were blinding, causing him to slow even more until they passed.

But now that pain in his chest again, it came full throttle. He was behind a snowplow and going slower, but at least he was protected from the oncoming lights. With one hand on the wheel, he was desperate to get his pills from his jacket pocket. Feeling for his jacket on the seat next to him, with one eye on the rear of the snowplow, he put his hand in the wrong pocket. The snowplow pulled over. He passed carefully with both hands on the wheel and plunged into the darkness. The snow, now falling in ever larger flakes, reflected the lights of his Jeep back at him, making it even more challenging to see where he was going.

Speaking his thoughts allowed, "I shouldn't be here. What the fuck am I doing, for Christ's sake." Now again, with one eye on the road, he searched for the pills but again got the wrong pocket. He was now in pain and agitated. He briefly took his eyes off the road, put his hand in the other jacket pocket, and found the pills. As he looked back up, a moose was in front of him, frozen in his headlights.

He jerked the wheel of the Jeep over. It swerved and went off the road down a small ravine to a lake. The car slid across the ice and came to a stop. There was the sound of ice cracking. He held his breath.

He had his heart pills firmly in his hand, unscrewed the lid, and tried to pop two into his mouth. In his hurry, he missed. The pills dropped somewhere in his clothing. There was another crack and a jolt, and he dropped the box. The pain in his chest was now excruciating. He was panicking, trying to pick up the box of pills and instinctively reaching for the door handle. In his head, he knew he needed to get out, but he needed to take his pills.

The Jeep filled with water and slipped slowly under. Darkness came about him as the car settled on the bottom of the lake. The outside temperature had dropped, and the snow continued for hours, maybe ten inches before daylight. By then, the Jeep's tracks through the woods down to the lakeside had become invisible.

Life can change in an instant. When we think we have our buttons all sewn on and everything under control, fate decides to take a different turn.

* * *

Time passed, and the weather changed, which excited the weather forecasters about the unusual weather hitting the coast of Maine. "It's crazy weather, folks," the weatherman on channel six smiled as the weather maps came up behind him. "Temperatures along the coast and inland are unseasonably warm." He described a warm front, enough to cause the ice in the lakes to melt much earlier than expected.

Later that same day, two boys, probably fourteen or fifteen years old, played with their dog. They were throwing sticks, just messing about, and after being stuck inside the house for most of the winter, were very happy to be outside with the thaw. They saw the outline of a car down two, maybe three feet below the lake water and about four from the lake's edge. They told their dad that night. They went to take another look the following day and decided to call the police, just in case. They knew the lake well; that car had not been there last year.

The car, a late model Jeep, was hauled out of the lake by local police. Inside, they found the body of a man in his sixties, and next to him, in a bag with some clothes and a wash bag, they found a German Walther p38 pistol and five thousand dollars neatly wrapped in one-thousand-dollar bundles.

They soon found Henry's driving license and contacted the Portland Police, who notified Caroline. The money and the gun raised more questions, but the police were tight-lipped about their theories. Henry's jeep was taken by truck to Portland, and the body of Henry Stern went to the Portland Medical Center morgue, where a pathologist established that he had died from a massive heart attack.

Decisions, Decisions, Decisions

It had been a week since Henry was cremated. The local papers in Portland, St John, and Quebec carried the story for about a day, and then it gave way to other news. At Caroline's request, a modest service was held for the family, a few friends, and the Stern Trucking and Shipping board. There was a private room to one side of the crematorium where people could talk, console each other, and speculate about what may have happened and, probably on most people's minds, what would happen now that Henry had passed.

Outside, on the street, a woman dressed in black did as best she could to remain unseen. She had traveled from Quebec. Her grief was as profound as any of the mourners inside the crematorium. Her life was turned upside down as events of the past unfolded and were out of her control. She had tried to stay away but was compelled to attend, even if she had to remain hidden. Just being there gave her a sense of closure.

Following the service at the Crematorium, everyone gathered at Henry's house. His ashes were placed on a wreath, which Caroline gently pushed into Casco Bay on an outgoing tide. The wreath had a photo of Henry and a card that read,

'Henry Stern. Dearly loved husband, father, and grandfather. A war veteran who fought bravely to help others.

* * *

With nothing else to do after leaving rehab, Robert had picked up where he had left off, working on the new office plans. He knew his design would never be built, but he needed to do something, even if it was just busy work serving to keep him occupied.

He lived at the Westin Portland Harbor View Hotel in the Portland Old Port. Among other things, it was famous for once refusing to allow Eleanor Roosevelt to stay for one night with her dog. It was close to the office, the container port at the western end of the docks, and just a fifteen-minute drive to the house he once shared with Caroline. Figuring this arrangement was temporary and only until they had a long-term agreement. Henry's house was an option until it was sold, but not one he wanted to take.

It had been a few days since Henry's funeral, and Caroline and Robert were home in the house he had designed and which they had built together. With a window behind them, they were sitting in high back wing chairs upstairs in the small library in the oversized hallway, a coffee table between them. Books on two walls surrounded them. Robert had now completed his treatment and committed to continuing weekly therapy sessions. He was taking Disulfiram, a drug that inhibited the ability to metabolize alcohol. One drink and you were 'as sick as a dog.' Caroline and Robert's dreams of growing old together now seemed remote and unlikely. The house was silent except for classical music; a clarinet concerto played quietly in the background. Their meeting today was to be a conversation Caroline had been avoiding.

It would be the first time they had a real opportunity to sit and talk since Robert completed the treatment and Henry's funeral.

They sat there, the coffee table between them, a physical barrier that underscored an emotional barrier. Caroline was on one side, and Robert was on the other. Caroline kept her distance and built an almost impenetrable wall around herself. Her face was motionless. "You can't come home," she told Robert.

Robert shifted uncomfortably and said, "I get it, I do, I do. I understand, but…"

Caroline slightly raised both hands and shook her

head. "Forget it, Robert. I find it hard enough to be here with you in this house even for an hour, never mind living here with you." And slightly squinting her eyes, "You betrayed my trust, and I don't see how I can ever forgive you. Your promises mean nothing to you, and I don't see how our lives can ever be the same. Too much has happened, and everything is different now."

Robert nodded in agreement, "I know. I know it will take time for you to trust me again, but I will prove it. I know you still love me".

Caroline ignored the question in the statement. She sat there looking straight at Robert without any apparent emotion.

Robert continued, "And in the meantime, I agree. I will continue to live at the hotel for now. I must think about what I want to do. I need to stay close to the kids, of course. I have learned a lot in the past weeks. A lot is still cloudy, but I remember more about what happened before. You know, when I was a kid. Sometimes,

I feel angry at my uncle for not telling me and avoiding questions. Honestly, Caroline, I know I will not turn to vodka ever again to help me deal with it. I am going to allow myself to feel whatever comes up."

Caroline nodded. She knew what he was talking

about.

"I've decided to take that trip I have talked about…, for as long as I can remember. I will find my roots and see if I can find out what my uncle would never share with me. I have talked about it for years, and now feels like the right time."

The conversation shifted. They talked about the kids, her new role at ST&S, and why the police still had not provided her with a complete picture of what had happened to Henry. Caroline said, "I have tried to get them to tell me what they know, but they are being circumspect. If they know why Dad was found dead at the bottom of a lake with a gun and bundles of cash, they are keeping it from me. All they are prepared to say is the autopsy showed he died of a heart attack. They do not have any suggestions as to why he was halfway to Canada driving on a night nobody in their right mind would even consider. But I suspect they know a lot more than they are telling."

Robert shared more information about what he had in mind, his planned trip to England, and the place of his birth. There was some talk about the kids and what the immediate plans were. She stood up, looked at him, gave a sort of shrug, and said, "Well, I guess that's it. I don't think there's much more to discuss just now." Robert took the cue, got up, and followed her to the front door. She gave him his coat and, just ever so lightly, touched his forearm and said,

"Goodbye, Robert."

He left in despair, feeling dismissed. He got in his car, pulled out of the driveway, drove around the corner, parked, and just sat there motionless, staring into space. Then, as if the ground was rumbling under his feet, his body shaking, it hit him like a landslide. With his head on the steering wheel, he sobbed uncontrollably.

The Next Best Thing

The mystery surrounding Henry Stern's association with Frank Lee remained. Eventually, we must come to terms with past tragedies and deal with life as it is now. Henry's disappearance deeply affected the Hall family; they seemed stuck in a 'time warp.' Caroline would feel the urge to pick up the phone and speak to her dad or start to think about Sunday lunch together. Her children would start a conversation about a memory of Henry, only to be overtaken by silence and a change of topic.

Caroline struggled to accept her new role at Stern Trucking and Shipping. Staying busy helped her to cope, but what Henry was doing driving to Canada, having left a note saying he would be going to Boston, continued to nag at her. It remained a mystery. She was now the head of ST&S and had pushed thoughts of a trip to Canada to the back of her mind. Her dad had been found, and following up on her leads was no longer relevant. Although she did need to visit the Quebec Terminal to give a personal update to employees and 'rally the troops,' she was in no immediate hurry. She kept putting the trip off with other things on her mind, leaving things to the local managers for now.

The board continued to support her, but she was pressured to decide the future direction for ST&S. What had been little more than a whisper some weeks back, now that Henry had been found, the conversation was front-and-center. Everyone agreed it was time to stop just treading water, and weighty decisions had to be made sooner rather than later.

Michael, being the oldest, was doing his best not to create problems at home and had been taking on more responsibility. Caroline marveled at how her oldest child, Michael, suddenly seemed to have grown up, like when spring turned to summer. As issues at the office increasingly required her attention, he told her, "Don't worry, you stay at the office. We can get our food. I will call if there are any problems and, by the way, we talked about it, we don't need to go to ski camp. We should stay home just in case." Ricky and Melissa nodded in agreement as they hung out in the kitchen over Breakfast.

"You should go," Caroline assured her three children, who had now miraculously become caring, gentle people. "A change of scenery will do you good. I love you guys." She encouraged them into a family hug, and all four became entwined – supporting each other through an impossible time.

Their lives were still on hold. No one could move on. It was too soon, and too much had changed. Michael, Ricky, and Melisa had developed a code between them. It worked sometimes, but not always. Never openly acknowledged, it was a barely visible pursing of their lips, eyes slightly widened, and a slight shake of their heads seemed to put an end to some, but not all, imminent explosions of emotion. Em had been around more than usual. She was supportive, ready to listen without judgment, and being there brought fresh air to the cloud hanging over the family.

* * *

It was late morning, and Caroline sat across the desk from Trevor Coulson, the Chief Financial Officer of Stern Trucking and Shipping, who had just filled and relit his pipe. Trevor, a balding man in his early sixties, stood about 6 ft, with brown eyes, a narrow face, and was skinny as a rake. He was a gentle soul who had been with the company for over twenty years and knew the ins and outs of the business. He was a trusted family friend. Their main concern now was what direction to take the company. Caroline waited as he lit his pipe.

"I love the sweet smell of that tobacco," she commented as she watched the first puff create a cloud around his head. It dissipated in the gentle breeze from the slightly opened window behind Trevor.

Trevor turned to the papers in front of him. "We are generally in good shape, but we are stuck. We need to address the future of the company and your role in it soon."

She interrupted him, "I know, but I just need a little more time to sort things out. Honestly, Trev, I am not sure what I want to do. Robert is out of rehab and going to Europe, and the kids are off to ski camp, so I will have time to myself and think."

"Right." Trevor agreed. "We are good for a week or two before we decide anything significant." Trevor was cautious and did not disclose his view of what Caroline should do. "Once you have decided, we should visit Canada to update the team. I can come with you and perhaps some other senior board members, depending on the decision. We must clearly state our financial position and outlook for the future."

Caroline agreed, "It's on my mind, and I should go, but as you say, after we are clear about the direction we need to go in."

Trevor continued, "Caroline, you have some options. You can maintain control and carry on as we are. You could still take the company public, which does not mean you will have to stay as Chairman. And, anyway, the banks may demand something else. I don't intend to be offensive, but while you are well respected, you are not Henry, and going public may no longer be an option.

"No, it's Okay, Trev. I appreciate your honesty. I could also sell to Global Shipping and avoid all the headaches."

Trevor responded, "They want to buy and have made a decent offer, and there may still be room for negotiation. As you know, they had started discussion before Henry...." he tailed off and then continued. "In the end, it's up to you, and I will do whatever is needed to support your decision, you know that."

"Yes. I know, and thank you. I will ponder a while and get back to you. Before doing anything, we should have an open and frank conversation about all the options with the rest of the board. Whatever I decide, it has implications for everyone, and they are all shareholders. Not to mention all the people on the payroll."

She stood and picked up the file Trevor had given to her at the start of the meeting.

Trevor said. "You do know that if you decide that selling is the best option for you, it will take some time to untangle things that your dad had in place. We operate in many jurisdictions and must determine management changes, finances, taxes, etc. You know the complications, but we will work with the lawyers to resolve it."

"Of course," replied Caroline as she opened the door.

Trevor got up from behind the desk and walked with her through the outer office, where a secretary was sitting, taking a phone call. They politely nodded to each other. Trevor watched Caroline as she turned from the door into the hallway, heading towards the office that used to be Henry's.

Caroline's brain was a mess, in overdrive. There was too much going on; still, she had not heard anything from Frank Lee. It was on her mind, but she was less concerned now that Henry had been found. While Frank Lee remained a mystery, she still had concerns and told herself that his secrets, whatever they were, should now remain hidden. However, sometimes, the warning that Frank Lee had given her that night on the phone in Boston still occasionally nagged at her. He had warned her, and she thought about it now; 'Someone will get hurt.'

She started to think about David Preston and that Sunday lunch. The discussion had been alarming, and while she had pushed it to the side of her mind, like the warning from Frank Lee, it was still there. But with so much to do in Portland, she told herself that was now in the past. At least, she thought it was. She was about to enter her office and decided to call David.

As she put her hand on the door handle, she

remembered he was on a plane today, heading for China on a trade mission due to the thawing of relations between the US and China. On an impulse, she turned around, walked to the elevator, headed down and out of the building, got into her car, and drove over the Casco Bay Bridge to South Portland, heading towards Henry's house on Cape Elizabeth.

Fifteen minutes later, she turned into the driveway, exited the car, and stood looking out across the now dormant gardens to Casco Bay. Soon, it would be spring, but today, everything was Gray. It was a gloomy day with wind coming in from the ocean. She stood, staring out to sea, the wind at her face like little needles pricking at her. She allowed a tear to roll down her cheek, wiped it with the back of her hand, and fished in her bag for the house keys.

* * *

Outside on the street, a small green truck stopped a few yards from the driveway entrance. The driver sat there, watching over the stone wall towards the house.

* * *

Once in the kitchen, she made some coffee and wandered with it around the house, still full of Henry's stuff. She opened doors to bedrooms, went in, opened closets, looked in the bathrooms and the medicine cabinets, just looking. Being so close to her dad's belongings, it was as if she somehow had not wholly lost him, and he was still there.

The house was as still as it had been when she

returned with Robert. That day, they found the note to Henry and the photo of the unknown woman. Both were lost when she was mugged, as Em had continued to insist whenever they talked about it. Caroline was not convinced it was a random opportunistic mugging.

On a whim, she opened a cabinet drawer and took out the notes she and Robert had made when they came to take another look around the house. She picked up the pen with the pad and perused the list. The pad had the name of a hotel, and the pen had the same logo printed on the side, 'Borderline Inn, Quebec, Canada,' with a phone number.

She went to the phone on the wall, picked up the receiver, and dialed the number.

"Bonjour, Borderline Hotel, ice et Claire."

"I am Caroline Stern." She deliberately used her maiden name,

"I am calling to find out if my dad, Henry Stern, ever stayed there. Maybe recently?"

Claire faltered, was silent, and quickly hung up the phone.

Caroline was about to redial when she heard someone calling from the front door. The voice called again, waited, and again, "Hello, Caroline, I need to talk to you." The voice repeated, "Hello, Caroline, I need to talk to you."

She heard footsteps on the wood floors and again, "Hello, Caroline?" The voice, she knew that voice. There was an accent. French? Maybe German? She turned around, grabbed her bag, and frantically searched for something. Frustrated, she turned it upside down. The manila folder Trev had given her earlier fell onto the kitchen island countertop, spread out, and its contents fluttered to the floor. She immediately saw the Mace pepper spray Em had given her following the Portland mugging,

Caroline got her thumb on the top of the spray and grabbed a large kitchen knife from the block. She looked back at the phone on the wall, judging if she had time to call someone, but she did not.

She held her breath as the kitchen door opened.

In L. L. Bean boots with jeans crumpled on top, wearing a shearing coat and a night watch cap on his head, a man very cautiously entered the kitchen and stood frozen as he looked at Caroline and said,

"I am Frank Lee. Will you help me?"

Can You Help Me

"Stop, stop right there," Caroline demanded as she quickly moved to grab the phone from its cradle on the wall. "Don't come another step closer. I know you attacked me in Portland!" She held the knife and the pepper spray higher in the air as if aiming.

Frank Lee put his hands up in front of himself with palms out. "What, no, I did not attack you. Not me! I promise. No, no, I do not mean any harm to you. Look, I will sit on the floor, and I am here to ask for help, not to attack you. Will you help me?"

Frank Lee sat on the floor and leaned back on the door jam. He stretched his legs out in front so Caroline could see the bottom of his boots. "I will not hurt you; I promise. I would never hurt you. You are Henry's daughter, and that means a lot. I promise. I am going to take my cap off, OK?"

Caroline nodded in agreement, noticing his balding head and the scar on his hand. She said, "What do you want? What do you know about my dad? Why has the FBI been looking for you? Why are you here?"

Frank Lee was sitting on the floor, looking up at

Caroline as he continued to plead with her. "I know you have questions, and I have thought to ask you for help many times over the past few weeks. And I want you to trust me. I understand. I have to tell you everything. But I worry about telling you what I Know. The past should be allowed to stay in the past. That is why I have not contacted you again since Boston. But now, I must. I have no other choice."

Caroline picked up the phone, "Don't you move. I don't know you, and there is no way I trust you."

"Don't call the police, please, no, don't call the police!

I BEG YOU."

"Why?"

Playing his only card, Frank Lee said, "If you want your dad to keep his good name, and David Preston too, you will not call the police. If you do, I will tell them what I know. You, your family, and your business will all be ruined. Please believe me. I am not lying to you."

Caroline put the phone down. "What are you talking about? And what has my uncle got to do with this? She put the knife down on the kitchen island counter, but it was still within easy reach as she moved in front of Frank. She had her back to the kitchen door, her escape route. She held the pepper spray in front of her. She pointed it at Frank like a gun with her thumb on the button, ready to press if anything threatening happened. She asked again, "What is going on?"

"Okay, I can tell you something and more after you help me, but you do not have to be afraid of me."

"What kind of help?"

"I need to get away, out of the country, and money. I will need some money."

Caroline backed away a couple of feet but stood there, staring.

Her mind was racing as she weighed him up. "So, this is about blackmail! I'll listen to what you want to tell me, but I'm not making any promises, and I'm certainly not staying here with you without someone knowing I'm here. I'm going to call a friend...."

Frank interrupted. "I wish you wouldn't, and this should be between you and me."

"No, if you want my help, I will take my chances on what you have on my family that is so damaging. I will call the person who was with me in Boston, and she knows as much as I do."

She stepped backward, keeping her eyes on Frank, picked up the phone from the cradle on the wall, and dialed Emily Whitt.

Frank mumbled, "Not a good idea," and reluctantly,

"OK." Em picked up, "Hi, this is Em."

"Em, it's Caroline, don't say a word, just listen. I am at my dad's house, and Frank Lee is here."

"WHAT! What are you saying? GET OUT NOW!"

Caroline had regained her composure and replied very calmly. "I need you to stay on the line, Em. Listen to the conversation. I need someone to know I am here and, so far, safe. He's asking for my help. I don't trust him, but he insists I am not in danger." She looked at Frank. He nodded and said, "Yes." It was loud enough for Em to hear.

"I promise," he said, opening his hand palm up,

"I will not harm you, and I need your help."

Caroline turned to Frank.

"How did you know my dad?"

"He helped me escape the war in Europe and provided me with papers and transport to get to America."

"Why did you want to meet with him?"

"The FBI is looking for me, as you know. If they find me, I will be sent back to Germany."

He left out a lot. He knew that if he had told Caroline everything at this stage, it would have set her against him. She would call the police, and he would have no chance of being helped and nowhere safe to run.

"I am a victim of mistaken identity," he said. "On the

news, there was a story about a woman who was arrested in Brooklyn, an ex-Nazi Guard. She had been hiding there for many years."

"I saw that." Caroline Said.

Frank Lee continued. "That woman approached me once in Boston when I was working and called me by another name."

"What name? What did she call you?"

"It wasn't my name, so I didn't pay much attention. It was a name I did not recognize, a German name, Moller, Herr Moller, or something like that. I told her she was mistaken, and she said she was sorry and walked away."

Now, listening to every word and watching Frank Lee closely, Caroline said, "So, what was your name before it was Frank Lee? That's not the name you were born with?"

"I am a Jew or used to be. My family and grandparents came from Prussia in the early nineteenth century, and they escaped the German Revolutionary War in 1819 and lived in Paris. We were happy until the Nazi occupation."

Em, on the phone, told Caroline, "This is a crock of shit. He is lying. I can tell, and I hear it in his voice."

Frank Lee continued his story, "They were taken to a death camp, but I managed to escape. Your Dad helped me.

Yes, I changed my name when I came to America and wanted to fit in. Then after that Nazi woman was arrested, strangers came asking questions, and I felt like I was being watched."

Caroline asked, "So why are you running from them? Why not just own up to being here illegally? You can probably get asylum."

"I am an illegal immigrant of German descent. The FBI came looking for me at Myrtle's. The bartender told me they gave him their card; it was someone from a Simon, something or other organization.

The bartender at Myrtle's promised to keep it to himself, but he told me. He is a good friend. I got scared and thought that if I had been mistaken for somebody else once, it could happen again, and I didn't know what to do. I hadn't seen Henry since he helped me escape to America, and I knew nothing about him. I never did contact him again. I thought about it last year after a story in the Boston Globe about his company. He had given an interview, but I never contacted him."

Frank figured he had satisfied Caroline and tried to move the conversation on. "I had promised not to, but then I needed help. I need help now, please."

"And? And what else?" asked Caroline.

158

"Things started to fall apart, and I sent your dad the story clipping. It was enough for Henry to get the message, and he met me in Boston a couple of weeks before he disappeared. I needed his help. I needed his help to get out of the country to Canada, Europe, or South America. He had ships, and I would need money to get started. Your dad was a good man. He helped many people, and perhaps there were some that he should not have, but it was the war. But now things have changed, and your dad was my only hope. I am so sorry he died, Caroline. It's terrible. I mean, the way it happened." He sounded sorry.

"I am scared."

"I can see that you are genuinely sorry, but it does not explain why you are trying to blackmail me to help you."

Frank responded, "I have told you what you need to know and answered your questions. It's the truth. I am not a danger to you. Your dad was going to help me get away on a container ship to South America or Australia, but he died. I am very sorry, but will you help me? I'm certain it's what he would want you to do. I was to be on a ship leaving Quebec at the new terminal there. Will you help me?"

All the while, Em listened and commented to Caroline in her ear, "It's a lie. Don't believe him. He's a con man. If you go along with this, with the FBI, you could be creating trouble for yourself. I am going to hang up now and call the police. Keep holding the phone so it appears that I am still listening." Em hung up the phone.

Caroline continued with her questions. "I will help you if you answer another question. What secret did you promise not to tell?"

"Well, it's something about your dad and David Preston."

"David, what's he got to do with this? What's this about?"

"I will tell when I am sure you will help me. Too many promises are broken, and I must be sure you will help." Frank Lee began to get up off the floor, "I want to leave now. Will you meet me?"

"Where?"

"In Canada," Frank said. "Quebec. The ships leave from there, and you could get me signed on as crew. That was the plan with Henry."

"Where in Quebec?" somehow, she knew the answer and held her breath.

"The Borderline Hotel in the Old Town." Caroline hesitated, "Why there?"

"There is a woman there, a friend of your father's. I will go there now and stay out of the way until you arrive. I have very little money, and she will help. Your dad helped her as well. She knows me and will happily let me stay there for a while." I was there waiting for your dad. He was going to help me, but the accident happened, and he never arrived. With nowhere else to go, I had to return to Boston. Now, you are my only hope to get away and a new life."

Caroline's mind was racing. "What is her name, the woman in the hotel?"

"It is Clair, Clair Lemoine. You will have to call her and ask her to help. I think she was important to your dad and will help, and I am certain she will cooperate once you tell her who you are and will keep it secret for sure."

Caroline was weighing her options, knowing the police were on their way; she was figuring out what to do. Here was a chance to get some answers, and almost as if somebody else was talking, she heard herself say, "I will help you, and I will meet you in Canada." She had no idea what she was talking about nor how to get someone onto a ship as crew and send them halfway around the world unnoticed.

Frank Lee quickly walked out the door, hurried down the driveway, out the gate, got in his truck, and drove away into the night. He was heading out to Route 95 on his way to Canada. The police arrived, and minutes later, Emily brushed past a police officer standing in the hallway and into the kitchen. Caroline stood at the kitchen counter talking to Sergeant Hope, stuff from her bag spread out before her.

"Thank god you are okay." Taking in the mess on the counter and papers on the floor, she said, "Caroline, you need to get somebody to clean up and do housework for you!"

Caroline explained her search for the pepper spray as she collected the papers and returned them to the folder.

Sergeant Hope commented, "You did the right thing. There is not much more we can do here this evening, and I would like you to come to Police HQ tomorrow to make a full statement." Em walked with them to the door and, returning to the kitchen, asked Caroline, "Are the Kids still at ski camp?" She nodded yes but did not say anything. "Robert?"

"He is on a plane to England searching for his past. He called me yesterday after he arrived. He was apparently in a hotel in Plymouth, near where he grew up. I spoke to him at lunchtime today. They are five hours before us, so the timing is awkward. He sounded weird. I hope he's not drinking."

"And David?" Em asked.

"In China, some trade deal thing. Spending taxpayer's money. Same old, same old. But I wish he was here. I have a lot of questions for him." Slowly, a possibility dawned on her. "Could he have possibly had me mugged, you know, for my clues, the ones I found in Henry's den?"

Em took a deep breath, screwed up her face, and with knitted eyebrows, "He knows something he's not telling, but having you mugged? That's a stretch, Caroline."

"I know, but then he was lying about Frank Lee. Remember he advised me not to turn over stones or something?"

Em, nodding in agreement, "You need a drink, my girl." She went to the fridge and found a bottle of Chardonnay.

"Yes, and a cigarette," she picked up a crumpled half-pack and matches from the mess on the countertop.

Em looked at her as she found a bottle opener in the kitchen drawer. "I want to learn more about what happened here, and, by the way, I thought we were supposed to be stopping that!" Caroline rolled her eyes as she offered the pack to Em.

The next day, Caroline told the police everything that happened. In exchange for agreeing to meet with Frank Lee and Clair Lemoine at the Borderline Hotel in Quebec, Caroline promised to keep Henry and David out of it, if possible. She agreed she would wear a transmitter wire and learn everything Frank and Clair knew.

Trip To Cornwall

Robert stepped off the plane from Boston at 7 a.m. and quickly passed through London Heathrow Airport immigration. Having completed all the paperwork and formalities and picked up a rental car from Hertz Auto Rental, he soon headed south along the A4 in search of his past.

He was driving cautiously on the left for the first time. It was tricky, but soon he settled down. Out on the motorway, trucks roared past him. They were smaller than the giant 18-wheeler tractor-trailers he was familiar with at home, but so were the roads. He turned the radio on and turned the tuning knob, and stopped when he heard a John Mayall album, So Many Roads. It seemed appropriate somehow. Robert turned up the volume and let the music fill the car and his head.

He followed the signs and took the A3 to Andover, where the highway ended. For the next 5 hours, he traveled on minor roads. The route passed through Exeter and then on to Plymouth. He got within a few miles of Plymouth, and jet lag finally caught up with him. It was late afternoon, and time to stop for the day.

He drove to the city's center without knowing exactly where he was going and found an old hotel with a comfortable room for the night.

The Duke of Cornwall was in the town center, a large old hotel built in the nineteen twenties. It had wrought iron balconies, railings, and a grand marble staircase. Inside, it was warm and welcoming. Under normal circumstances, the architecture would have held his attention as he climbed the few steps into the hotel. But now, it mattered little to Robert. It had been a long journey, and he was exhausted. He checked in, got his key, and headed to the stairs, steering clear of the welcoming bar just off the reception area. He knew that just one drink would make him feel sick, and he could easily be back on the sliding road from which, this time, there would be no turning back. He knew that if he ever had a chance of Caroline forgiving him, he had to stay sober for the rest of his life.

With his suitcase in one hand and his leather bag with a shoulder strap on his left shoulder, he walked up the marble stairway and along a hallway to his room. He went in, dropped the shoulder bag on the bed, placed his suitcase on the stand in the corner, and took in his surroundings. The room was simple yet elegant. It had a four-poster bed, matching heavy wood furniture, a closet, a chest of drawers, a comfortable chair, and an updated modern bathroom. From the window, there were sweeping views out across the city. He looked at his watch and decided to call Caroline. It was 3:30 p.m. England time, making it 10:30 a.m. on the East Coast. Sitting on the bed, he picked up the phone from the side table, dialed 0 for the hotel operator, and gave her the number.

The phone rang six or seven times before the answering machine picked it up. "Hi, this is Caroline and Robert. Please leave a message, and we will return your call soon."

Hearing her voice comforted Robert, especially since she had not changed the greeting. It was like sitting in a warm bath, allowing your aches and pains to dissipate. Robert took a couple of deep breaths, pushed back the lump in his throat, and left a message: "Hi Caroline, sorry to miss you. It's 3:30 in the afternoon here, and I'm exhausted and going to nap before dinner. Maybe we can speak later, or I will try again tomorrow."

Robert put the phone back in its cradle and sat motionless with images of Caroline and the kids eating breakfast and now off on their daily routines. It was all fantasy, his imagination nudging him. He sat on the edge of the bed for a couple of minutes, looking at the phone, his only connection back to the people he loved.

He was feeling sorry for himself. He was alone in a foreign land, and even though he had not reached his destination, he wondered if he should give up and go home. He got up, went to the bathroom, looked at himself in the mirror, and said, "You look like shit." He took a shower, slid semi-nude between the sheets, and fell asleep.

Somehow caught between dreaming and being half awake and uncertain as to which, he had visions of his house as a child of nine, waking up at night, getting out of bed, and looking out of the window. Then, unconscious in a deep sleep, he was tossing and turning with voices in his head.

"Robert, wake up now, wake up. Are you okay?"

He was awake, heard voices, and sat up in bed. People outside his bedroom door made a noise as they opened the door to their room next door. The voices subsided, and he drifted back to sleep and into the dream world.

People were running. A ladder appeared, and he tried to climb it but could not lift his foot off the ground. He was stuck. It was one of those dreams when you know you are dreaming, and somehow, in the exasperation of being unable to move, you wake up. He lay in the dark, running the dream in his mind's eye. The images changed to more recent memories of Caroline's anger, the kids playing catch in the yard, the ski trips, and the drinking. In his imagination, he saw the bottle he kept in his desk drawer or used to. The last one he remembered, Caroline, had poured away. His thoughts swirled as he said aloud to the darkened room, "I let you and the kids down, Caroline. But it's over now, and I will prove it to you."

He drifted into a tortured sleep, the returning dreams holding him in memories of a dark past. The sound of the ocean, a child crying, people shouting, and a phone ringing woke him up; he rolled over and reached the bedside table to search for the phone. Finding it, he nearly dropped it, and now more awake, he put the phone to his ear and said, "Hello."

"Robert, it's Caroline. Should I call back later?"

"No... no, I need to wake up." He looked at the clock next to the bed. "It's just after 6 pm here, lunchtime there, I guess?"

Rubbing his eyes, he sat up in bed, "Okay, I am awake."

"Is everything okay?" Caroline asked.

"Just thought to let you know I arrived, and well, err, I am staying at this hotel, the Duke of Cornwall, in

Plymouth." His head was still groggy, "Well, obviously, you know that because you called me."

"Are you okay? Did you have a drink?"

"Oh no, I am done with that, no," he answered truthfully. "It's just the jet lag. I was sleeping. It is the time difference, that's all. Kids Okay?"

"They are at ski camp."

"Oh, right, of course, my head's just a bit fuzzy from the sleep, the jet lag...."

"Well, okay, all is good here," Caroline responded. "Glad you arrived okay."

"I miss home," Robert said. He waited, hoping for a positive response and that she would say she missed him too and wanted him to come home. Instead, there was silence.

"Well, okay, I'm going now. I will get something to eat, check in with the office, and have an early night. I have a busy day tomorrow." And in a dry, flat tone, "Bye, Robert."

"Bye, Caroline, see you soon." But it was too late, and she had already hung up. He had hoped for something more, perhaps an indication that she missed him and a possibility, a suggestion of a chance they could get back together.

He got out of bed, dressed, and went to the lobby for

food. Going straight to the restaurant, carefully avoiding the bar, he was shown to a table overlooking the street. He sat just looking through the window while mentally barely acknowledging a car struggling to park in an almost too-small space. He was staring into the darkness when the voice in his head called to him. "Robert, wake up."

He came out of his reverie as the waiter arrived and took his order for soda water with ice and lemon, followed by shepherd's pie, peas, and potatoes. It was OK, nothing special, and he wondered why the Brits were keen on it. He made a mental note not to order it again. He finished dinner and went to the front desk to ask questions about distances and the travel times tomorrow.

The concierge was helpful. He was an older man, perhaps in his fifties, five feet eight or so, a bit rotund. He wore a black jacket, a red tie, and a welcoming smile. His name badge proudly stated he was Eric Howell.

"How long to travel to Penzance, Eric," he asked.

Eric picked up a map from under the desk and pointed, "Take the A 39. It is about two hours, three if traffic is bad, but mid-week, you should not have any problem, especially at this time of year. It's a nice drive. If you leave after breakfast, you can be there for lunch. I can recommend a hotel if you plan on staying."

"I will be there for three or four nights, thanks. I also need some information about the area, especially Penzance."

Eric loaded him with brochures for sightseeing: beaches, Churches, old tin mines, historic buildings, restaurants, and additional maps for towns in the general area.

Robert thanked him. Feeling the need for fresh air, he stepped from the hotel, turned left, and wandered along Citadel Road to Plymouth Hoe Park and the Promenade, looking out across the bay to the English Channel towards the islands of Guernsey and Jersey with France beyond. Of course, he could only see them in his imagination, and he could only see them from what he had learned by looking at maps. The wind was blowing onshore, and the air felt damp, very different from Maine's cold, dry winter air. Something in Robert stirred. It was a feeling, a familiarity yet elusive. It was just beyond the reach of his consciousness.

Later, he slept fitfully. The dreams were now vivid. He woke up many times and lay half asleep, thinking about what he remembered of his childhood. He had a feeling of a dream or a memory, just beyond clarity. You know something is there but can't get ahold of it. It was like his earlier feeling when looking out across the ocean. There was some familiarity about it.

He remembered hearing voices and seeing searchlights piercing the sky, looking for planes from Germany. It was wartime. He recalled playing in the garden, running for cover when the sirens blasted out the warning that an air raid was imminent.

He remembered fresh eggs from the chickens in the yard of the house he grew up in. He knew his parents' faces from an old black and white photo his uncle had given him, with them all in their Sunday best clothes.

An angry feeling seemed to possess him. It had been this way for as long as he could remember. A seething that would occasionally rise, he would push it away with a stiff drink, not wanting to be that person and afraid of what he may do. Robert had never wanted to share this dark side, and Caroline had only ever seen glimpses of it, not sufficient to be concerned, and she certainly never felt it directed at her.

His anger at the world waited silently in the shadows of his mind, waiting for an expression, a release. It was a familiar feeling he came to know in therapy. Robert admitted the unacknowledged resentment towards his uncle, who always seemed to be hiding something of the past from him, never telling him the whole story of when and how he came to be in America. Anger at Caroline for constantly nagging him about his drinking and his anger at himself for doing work that never really satisfied his ambition to do something special. His resentment towards Henry, who was often cold towards him and who gave him what Robert called the 'family obligation work.' Scant images swirled in his mind as tears trickled down his cheeks.

Go out of the front gate, turn left along the path, and go up the hill. Then there is nothing, and everything is a blank. What happened? He could not remember. Unsure if he was dreaming, he realized he was awake. He turned and tried to sleep again but was restless, and sleep was elusive.

He got out of bed, sat at the desk, and used the notebook to jot down design ideas, a practice that had served him well as an architect. He wrote notes and drew small pictures of what he could remember about the house he lived in with his parents. He stayed there, lost in his work, until four in the morning. Finally, he put the pencil down, closed the book, and returned to bed. He slept soundly for the next three hours.

The next day, Robert soon found his way back onto the A38. The day was bright and sunny, traffic was light, and the road ahead was clear. While his usual companion in the car was a feeling of dread, he felt hopeful this morning. Caroline was constantly on his mind. He wished he could share with her his recollections of yesterday. But knowing she wasn't interested, he pushed the urge to call her to one side. Slowly turning the dial on the car radio, he stopped when he heard Elvis Presley singing 'Only the Lonely.'

Aloud and to himself, "Yup, that's me."

Then, much to his surprise, the disc jockey broke in with a station announcement.

"This is Tony Blackburn, and this is Radio Caroline."

He grimaced, lips pressed together, eyes narrowed. His hands tightened on the wheel as he stepped harder on the gas, 70, 80, 85, and 90 miles an hour. In the back of his mind, a voice called, 'Robert, wake up, wake up!'

He came to his senses and eased off the gas. In his mind, he could see Caroline as she told him two days before he checked into rehab the second time, "I can't live with you anymore. This so-called illness is all self-inflicted. I can't be your nurse any longer. I am done nursing you."

Driving along the A38 in England, away from everything that anchored his life, Robert's sadness welled up. He was a broken man on an emotional roller coaster with more hurdles to cross and inner challenges to face. How would he ever resolve the sadness of losing his family again? He was the lost child from England who is now grown up and living in the shadow of his past. Reflecting on how Caroline had forgiven him before, in his heart of hearts he firmly believed she wanted to keep the family together. Maybe he could turn things around.

Then, feeling deeply sorry for himself, out loud, he said, "I should kill myself. It should have been me, not Henry. They would all be better off." Suddenly, he was nauseous, and the feeling was about to overcome him. He pulled off the road onto a grassy shoulder, stopped, opened the car door, leaned over with his head out, and vomited. He took deep breaths and a swig of water from the bottle in the cup holder before re-starting the engine and driving back onto the A38, seeking his past to resolve the present.

After All These Years

St. John, New Brunswick, Canada 1964

There had been a strike at the terminal in St John. The staunch union members were against those that were not, and minor fights broke out. It was no more than pushing and shoving as people aired their differences.

Henry understood how feelings could run hot, which tempered his approach. He soon reached an agreement with the Unions. It had been a tough week and a trying day. With a new contract agreed upon, people could get back to work, and he could now move forward with expansion plans.

Sometimes, when Henry needed to clear his head, he would wander the St. John City Market, a four-story red brick building. He liked being among these people, reminiscent of those he grew up with in Van Burren, Maine, on the border with Canada. Nestled along the Saint John River in Aroostook County, the town's History is deeply intertwined with the lumber and railroad industries, which

176

were instrumental in shaping Henry's growth and development as a young man before the war drew him into Europe.

The St John City Market had many vendors selling household goods, flowers, fabrics, pots and pans, and an ever-changing array of clothing that changed with the seasons.

The enclosed structure captured the aromas of the food stands, stimulating the senses as they wafted through the market. Music from loudspeakers meshed with people gathering and meeting with friends while their children were at play, running up and down, their high-pitched voices contributing to the milieu. They reminded him to stay close to his grandchildren while they were young and full of energy and enthusiasm.

The atmosphere was grounding for Henry. It was a delicious assortment of humanity. He loved it and would stop at one of the food wagons to get coffee and breathe it all in.

The development of the terminal was big news for the small town, and it made the front page of the local newspaper, along with a photo of Henry. Although he was older and not as lean as he once was, Claire was almost sure this man was the one she loved—the man who had saved her from peril.

The day after the article about the agreement with the union appeared in the newspaper, To clear his head, Henry decided to walk to the market and was sitting at a table sipping coffee when Claire wandered through the market on her way to work. She froze when she saw him. She had been trying to push the photo in the newspaper from her mind. But there he was, drinking coffee and reading through a wad of white pages, a document of some sort. She stood back, mostly concealed behind one of the market stalls, and watched Henry for five minutes, observing his mannerisms, checking to ensure she was not mistaken. She was convinced it was him. In her head, she was arguing with herself as to whether or not to approach him. The decision, however, was made for her as he finished his coffee, got up, and wandered away. She followed him, being sure to stay well behind him. The market was busy, and she lost sight of him in the crowd. She told herself to let it go, that is, until the following day.

Claire worked as a housemaid at the St John Hilton Hotel, where Henry stayed on his visits to the Canadian Terminal. Following a failed marriage, she left New York years ago and moved to St John. She lived in a small apartment in town, close to the open-air market. While not super luxurious, the St John Hilton Hotel had decent rooms that looked out over the water. Henry had stayed there many times since developing the Canadian Yard. Buying the yard was risky, but he had worked hard to develop it. Henry wanted to be number one in North America, and the St John Terminal was a crucial asset to Stern Trucking and Shipping's goal of becoming a global company.

On a whim or an instinct, Claire wondered if, by chance, Henry was staying at the hotel. She checked hotel records, and much to her surprise, He was a guest. Then, during her break, Claire returned home and got a photo of herself taken a couple of years ago. Returning to the hotel to continue her shift, she opened the door to Henry's room with her passkey. She left her service trolley outside the door, entered, scanned the room, and closed the door behind her. The bed was unmade, and used towels were thrown on the tub's edge. There was screwed-up paper in the waste basket. A couple of the hotel's give-away pens and an open black leather-bound folder were on the desk.

Opening the closet, she ran her hands over his jacket and gently touched a couple of shirts on hangers. She put her face on the jacket and smelled again the person she remembered from so long ago. She closed the closet door, moved to the desk, and noted the glass of water to the right of the black leather folder. She carefully observed the angle of the pens to the folder, not touching anything. She studied what was written, just a list of things to do. She took in the writing and noticed how the dot above the I was not in the right place, more to the left over the preceding letter. She had been trained as an analyst, then coerced as a specialist, working for the Nazis when she was Bette Caron.

Back then, while not feeling safe, she had been doing work she loved, studying details, and making sense of things that first appeared to make no sense. But she also hated the world she had lived in so many years ago.

She turned from the desk and looked in the dressing table drawers, quietly observing how neat things were: socks, underwear, sweaters, and gloves. It was in Henry Stern's nature to leave things tidy and to bring order to a world that otherwise fell to pieces.

She turned to the door, opened it, and pulled her trolley halfway in, using it to keep it open and stop anybody from catching her unawares. She did her work, cleaned the bathroom, placed fresh towels and toiletries, folded the end of the toilet paper, emptied the trash, vacuumed, and made the bed. She then stood at the desk, looking at Henry's notepad and the list of things to do. For a while, she was stuck and could not move as she conjured up what she wanted to say.

Picking up a pen, she wrote below his list. "Henry, do not be alarmed. I had no idea until yesterday when I read the newspaper that you are here. Here is my address and phone number." She wrote them carefully to ensure they were legible. Here is my photo. "If you wish, you can contact me. If you do not contact me, I will never bother you. I will leave this job and St. John. The last thing I want is to put you in a difficult position because, Henry, I will never forget what you did for me." She wrote the exact words on the back of the photo and signed the note, Claire Lemoine.

She put the pen down and carefully placed the photo next to her note. She collected her cleaning supplies, quietly left, and moved on to the next room on her schedule.

Henry found Claire's note later that afternoon. He sat down at the desk with the photo in his hand. His heart remembered everything. He remembered the passion, the urgency of the romance, a touch, a certain look. He thought of his now-deceased wife. He had lived alone since she died and became very focused on the business. He had not noticed how the years were wearing on him. When Henry saw the photo, those years evaporated. He came alive, his heart raced, and his body tingled like an adolescent.

None of us know what fate awaits us. Life has a funny way of putting people on our path. And then, some who were so important to us are gone. We each move on and make new friends, and the memory of those other friends, lovers, allies, and enemies disappear into a fog of images and feelings.

When we take time, we can peer through the fog and remember a look, a conversation, or a feeling of what we were doing at the time. Sometimes, those memories are stimulated by music, a half-remembered conversation, or a situation similar to past experiences. They remind us of those times, those other people. We were younger then. Then you meet again, and all the old memories come flooding back. "Do you remember this? And remember the time when we did such and such. Did you ever hear from so and so, and I wonder what ever happened to…"?

* * *

At first, he felt awkward and unsure. They both did. Waiting for their table, they sat at the bar of a restaurant in the downtown area of St. John. Henry had a Dewar's scotch on the rocks, and Claire had a glass of Merlot. They talked for hours about when the world was at war. They could be killed by a Nazi bomb anytime and lived as though their death was imminent. Hearts were free then. The future was uncertain, and people did not worry much about tomorrow. The social restrictions of the early nineteen hundred had dissipated. People mainly lived in the present, and falling in love was easy. People would meet, strangers would become friends, and spend time together, not knowing if this day would be their last.

* * *

Over the following year, they would see each other whenever Henry was in St. John. She maintained her independence; it was important to her. Regardless, for Henry, money was not an issue in his life. Nevertheless, while he had made a difference in her ability to pay her bills, she continued her work at the hotel.

* * *

Claire LaMoine stepped from the shower and came into the room with a towel around her head, tying the belt on the hotel dressing gown. Henry was sitting on an easy chair next to the window, wearing a pair of slacks and a white shirt undone at the collar. He had one sock on and was about to put the other on his left foot. He looked up and smiled at her. She saw him smiling and teasing him a little, "You look pleased with yourself."

He put the other sock on as she moved towards him, bent over, and kissed him on the forehead.

Henry said, "How would you like to own a hotel of your own?"

Claire stood back, surprised, "Oh, I don't think so. That would be tough, hard work, and take all my time."

"Yes, but no harder than what you do now. And, anyway, you would have staff and be your own boss."

She sat on the bed's edge, putting her head to one side as if to ask a question. Henry moved from the chair, sat beside her on the bed, and explained.

"It's in Quebec, in the center of the old city. It's been on my mind for a while. Just like you," he put his arm around her shoulders and kissed her gently. Then, with a more serious expression, "I've looked at it several times. It's for sale. I got their financial reports last week when I was there at the container terminal. I have thought about it a lot. It would be entirely in your name. There would be renovations, and we would have to figure out new marketing and probably change the name. But I promise, no strings. It would be yours."

Clair shook her head, "I don't know, Henry, it is a big commitment, and I don't think I could let you do that. As good as it sounds, I don't see how I...."

Henry interrupted, "Don't overthink it. I want to buy it for you. Say yes!" He quickly added, "There is a nice owner's apartment, and I have looked all over it. They speak French, of course! Say Yes!"

Clair smiled and took his hand in hers, "I would prefer to be in Portland with you. It makes me sad, but I know it can't be."

Henry removed his hands from her gentle touch, turned and pulled her towards him, and hugged her. She responded. They held each other for a minute, allowing their warmth to flood over and be absorbed by them.

Henry released her from his embrace, turned and cupped her face in his hands, and looked into her eyes. "I know, and I want you to be in Portland with me as well, maybe one day." Repeating himself, "Maybe one day."

There was a brief silence." I love you, Claire, but you would be under too much scrutiny in Portland, and it could be dangerous."

"I know it." she said, "And I love you right back."

Hospital Visit

Cornwall 1974

Robert stopped in the center of Penzance, leaned over the back of the car seat, grabbed the leather shoulder bag, hauled it over to the front, and tossed it on the passenger seat next to him. Opening the flap, he pulled out his notebook, flipped back a few pages, and checked the Hospital's address. Picking up the map that was open on the dashboard, he soon found the West Cornwall Hospital on St Clare St, just a few minutes away.

* * *

Having completed written inquiries to the hospital a few weeks earlier when recovering, Robert found where he used to live as a child. It was somewhere in or near Penzance, Cornwall, England. He had called the hospital and was put through to Maria Dawson, the Senior Administrator at the West Cornwall Hospital.

"Oh, thanks for calling Mr. Hall. I have good news for you! We searched, and I am glad we found some information about you in the files. Give me your address, and we will send it to you.

"That's great, but no need to mail it. I am planning a trip to England. I want to see where I grew up! I've been planning this trip for a long time, and I have never been to England, well, not since I was a child. After leaving the hospital, my uncle brought me to America when I was about ten."

"That will be fine," she replied. "It will be here when you arrive."

Robert asked a few questions about what was in the file and the hospital's address. He was about to hang up when he remembered something. "Oh, one more thing, is there, by chance, an address in the file where I lived at the time?"

"Hold on. I'll take a look." Thirty seconds later, Maria came back on the line. "Yes." She gave him the address and thought he had misunderstood.

"I am sorry, Maria, but would you mind spelling that." He repeated each letter to ensure he had it as he wrote in the notebook before him. M- O -U -S -E- H- O- L- E

"Really? I lived in a place called Mouse Hole!"

Maria Dawson laughed. "I know! We pronounce it 'Muzzle, like what you put on a dog! But for strangers, we always spell it out so they don't get lost trying to find us. We have a very nice little harbor popular with tourists in the summer. It's about two and a half miles from Penzance. The coastline is rugged, and it has quite a history. Back to the thirteen hundreds."

"Well, thank you so much. I look forward to meeting you in due course." He hung up the phone, looking at the paper before him. "Mousehole, who knew! An asshole from Mouse Hole." He was smiling.

* * *

Robert was sitting in the car, remembering details and looking at the map. His depressed mood had lifted slightly. Coming out of his reverie, he closed his notebook, picked up the shoulder bag, and went to the hospital entrance. He walked through the wrought iron gate with an overhead arch to the door into a foyer and the reception desk and asked for directions to find the senior hospital administrator.

Maria Dawson was expecting him. As he entered the room, she stood up and moved from behind her desk to greet him. She was in her mid-forties, with dark hair cut short with red highlights and a row of beads around her neck. She offered Robert her hand with several rings on three of her fingers. They shook hands, and Maria pointed to a chair and invited Robert to sit down.

"I have everything here for you." She moved to her side of the desk, sat down, and opened a red folder set to one side atop a pile of papers, more folders, and books.

"I am glad we talked before you made your trip. This stuff was not easy to find. It was tucked away in the corner of our archives, which are a bit of a mess. There is talk of computers, but that's probably years away."

Robert took a seat. "Well, I appreciate that you made an effort. The records are important to me. I was born in, how do you say it? Muzzle"

"Close enough." She smiled.

Robert continued, "I have no real memory of my life before I moved to the U.S.A. when I was just barely ten years old,"

For the next 20 minutes, Robert and Maria went through the file together. There were handwritten notes about how he was brought to the hospital and remarks about what had happened. Robert could not remember any of it, as his memories of that time were still vague.

"Well, that's about it," said Maria. "Didn't your uncle ever tell you more about all of this?" as she pointed to the file.

Robert shrugged and shook his head. "No, he never did tell me, then he died suddenly in a car accident. It was a hit-and-run. Unfortunately, the driver was never found. My uncle's wife, my aunt, is American and knows nothing of our history. I did ask, but it was as much a mystery to her as it was to me. She moved to San Francisco after my uncle died, and I don't get to see her much anymore."

"That's too bad." Maria quickly added, "I mean that he died, of course." She changed the subject, "If you go to the police in town, you can meet my friend Chief Inspector Jago Cooper. He was a constable back then and may be able to give you more information. I'll let him know you have spoken to me."

Robert stood up. "Thank you so much. I don't know if I would have gotten this far without you, and it's appreciated." He pointed to the file, "May I take copies?"

"Of course, I copied them for you." Maria got up, shook his hand, and assured him she was available if he needed anything more. She called after him as he left the room, "Happy hunting, Robert."

He returned to the rental car and saw Maria watching him from the window. As he got in, he waived, but she pulled away. She most probably didn't see him. After studying the map, Robert left the car park and headed towards Newlyn.

From there, he followed Fore Street onto Cliff Road, heading towards Mousehole and his past.

I Used to Live Here

With its raucous history of pirates and smugglers, Mousehole had been a fishing village since the fourteenth century. Its protected harbor had a little beach where the voices of children playing would compete with the squawking seagulls in the summer.

Robert wandered the crooked, narrow streets, taking in the architecture and, along with some out-of-season visitors, window-shopped. There were a few art galleries, a grocery store, and unique one-of-a-kind stores selling gifts and souvenirs. There was also a delightful tea shop where it was just an unwritten rule that visitors must stop at least once to sample a famous Cornish cream tea.

Sitting on the harbor breakwater stone wall, with fish and chips wrapped in the traditional newspaper, Robert ate with his fingers, tossing an occasional treat to the seagulls who were relentless in their demand for food. They fought with each other over every tiny scrap he threw at them. Some fishing boats and a few small sailboats were pulling restlessly on their mooring lines, waiting for low tide when the harbor would drain out, and the boats would sit as if resting, waiting for the next tide.

It had been about thirty years since Robert had lived there, and the village had not changed much. The old schoolhouse was up on the hill overlooking the harbor, and narrow streets surrounding the harbor lined with white-painted houses with slate roofs. All were a treat in Robert's architect's eye. One could imagine that the homes built in the hills surrounding the harbor would have had stunning views of the village and the harbor in one direction and across hills and meadows in another.

The sea wall, where Robert was eating his lunch, ran parallel to the road and reached the end of the town, where it faded into hedgerows. Robert remembered the stony beach as his playground during the war. He recalled the geography, the coves, and the rocky shoreline beyond the village. Having finished his lunch and tired of wandering the tiny streets, Robert sat in his car for a while, looking out to sea, recalling the sound of the sirens screaming warnings of an attack by German airplanes. The urgency of those sirens would have him running back up the hill onto the farm road that led to his house.

He had been putting it off, nervous about returning to the home he had to leave as a child. Finally, he picked up his leather bag from the passenger seat, exited the car, and walked out of the village along a road with hedges to the right and a sea wall to his left. He turned right when he came to the farm road, and there it was, on the right, about 500 feet from where he turned. It was smaller than he had remembered. There was a vegetable garden in the front and a small farm out back where he now recalled chasing chickens around the yard in his childhood and helping his mom milk the cow. The cow shed had been modified but still had much of the old wood. It now had parking spots for two cars.

An image came to Robert's mind. He remembered carving his name on one of the beams and wandered into the building. Looking up to the corner of a support beam, he saw his name. He had carved it with the scout's jack knife his dad had given him. A door to his memories was slowly being pried open. He had a queasy feeling in his stomach as he remembered more of the time he had lived there. Perhaps now, the long-lost key to the door of his memories was found, and the door was slowly opening.

"Can I help you?"

Robert was startled as he looked around to see a

woman, probably in her sixties, standing there. "Oh," Robert hesitated, "I am Robert." He blurted out. "There look, in the wood. That's me. I carved my name there when I was just a kid. During the war, I lived here."

He walked towards her, holding out his hand. "I'm sorry. I should have knocked and asked to come on your property, but I used to live here." Instead of offering her hand in return, she put some turnips in his hand. She had been gardening and removing the winter root vegetable crop.

"Do you like turnips?" she said with a slight grin appearing on her lips. "They seem to grow so well around here, can't cook enough or give them away."

Robert smiled. "I am sorry," and quickly added, "but not about the turnips, but about intruding."

"Oh, that's okay." And eyeing him carefully, "I am Peggy, Peggy Messa. It's an old Cornish name, and it means to gather acorns." And still smiling, "Although why I would have a name that means to gather acorns is beyond me. Want some tea?"

Robert, hesitating, said, "Thank you, but I do not mean to intrude."

"Think nothing of it. Visitors are always welcome. You're American, right?" Not waiting for him to reply and pointing towards her front door, she said, "Come on in. I'll put the kettle on. Watch out for the beast. He will lick you to death."

With a big old Welsh Collie napping on the floor next to her, Peggy served tea and scones with cream and jam while Robert described the reason for his visit.

"Just visiting my past," he told her.

They talked about shared memories of the house, the war, people she knew, and some who had never returned. She showed him photos of herself and her now-deceased husband.

"Yes, sad, he died in the war. We both grew up in Penzance. I miss him. We lost a good few here, including your mum and dad. But that time has passed, and we all have to get on with our lives, I suppose." As she poured more tea for Robert, she continued. "I did not know your parents. I moved into the cottage about fifteen years ago, early retirement from teaching school to ten-year-olds."

Peggy took Robert on a tour of the rest of the house. All the while, she described how the place used to be and the changes she had made. Robert struggled to remember much of it. They returned to the kitchen, and Robert picked up his leather shoulder bag and got ready to leave.

"You should also go and have a chat with Margaret. She is the postie. If anyone remembers what happened here, back in the war days, then Margaret Pengelley is the person you need to speak to!"

As Robert left, clutching the turnips and another scone Peggy had pushed into his hand, she called out, "Be sure to tell Margaret I sent you and to remember we have a council meeting tomorrow!"

Thanking her again, Robert said, "I will be sure to tell her, and thanks again." Then, with a grin, holding up the turnips and scones she insisted he should have, he said, "Thanks so much for your hospitality."

He put the scones and turnips in his bag, found his way from the cottage to a pathway across the hillside, and stood there looking out to sea across the English Channel towards France. Clouds were forming, and it was getting late, and it was time to call it a day.

I Remember You

Robert was soon back in the rental car, figuring out the direction he should go. He alternately looked at his map and the hotel brochure given to him by the concierge yesterday. A man in a dark uniform with a yellow band around his hat, book in hand, knocked on the window—a Traffic Warden. Robert wound down the window. "You can't park here, mate, yellow lines," he pointed to the sidewalk.

"Err, sorry," Robert said. "I am just looking for the Old Coast Guard Hotel." He held up the map.

"The Coasty is up Parade Road. It's a bit more than a mile away. Here, let me show you." And taking the map from Robert, "See, it's here. You'll have to turn around and go up North Cliff Road past the Post Office, then left on Commercial Road and right on Parade Hill. It's going to be up on the right. You can't miss it. It's nice with views across the bay to St Michael's Mount."

"Okay, thanks," Robert said, relieved he did not get a ticket. He looked again at the map and headed off searching for 'The Coasty.'

The Old Coast Guard Hotel was a small white stucco building with a wrought iron fence on either side of the four steps that led to a pale blue entrance door with wood trim faded a little and battered by the sea. The Hotel was a collection of buildings annexed to the original over the years. Robert parked the car in the little side yard of the hotel, got his suitcase and shoulder bag, and walked along the narrow sidewalk up the stairs to the reception, where he received a warm welcome.

"Good afternoon, sir. How can I help you?" Asked a twenty-something young woman with a black skirt, white shirt, and hair tied back in a ponytail.

"Robert Hall, I have a reservation for three nights."

Looking at the register, "Yes, we have a room for you that overlooks the sea. It has a small balcony. I hope you will like it." Robert completed the paperwork, and the receptionist handed him a key. She pointed, "Room eleven is to the right and up the stairs. At the top, turn left, and you will find it just down the hallway."

Unlocking the door, he put his suitcase and shoulder bag on the bed. Pushing the curtains aside, he opened the window and took a deep breath as he gazed out onto the bay and St. Michael's Mount, a small island with a building up on a hill. St. Michael's Mount was accessible by boat at high tide and by foot at low tide. Robert later learned about the now-disused underground narrow-gauge railway from New Harbor. Built in the previous century, it ran for about six miles. It was once the only way to transport legitimate and smuggled goods to and from the tiny island.

Robert picked up a local guide from the shelf that formed part of the bed headboard, kicked off his shoes, stretched out on the bed, and began reading. He promptly fell asleep.

He woke up an hour or so later, about 5:30 for Robert and 12:30, lunchtime at home in Maine. He sat up, picked up the phone from the small table next to the bedside table, dialed the operator, and gave her the number. Caroline's phone rang, he was anxious, and his stomach was a bit queasy. He hoped she would pick up, but the call went to the answering machine.

"I just thought I would check in with you. How is everything? The kids, you? Call me if you have received this before about six o'clock in your time. It will be eleven here, but I may be asleep by then. Call anyway; I am at the Old Coast Guard Hotel near Penzance."

That night, Robert had dinner at the hotel's bar. He was testing himself to see if he could stay away from alcohol. He was proud of himself for being able to go to a bar with others around him drinking. Robert ordered a tonic of water. He struck up a conversation with a couple visiting from London. They shared experiences and talked about their families and why they visited this part of England.

Following a restless night, he awoke feeling drained and still tired. He took a shower and dressed before returning to the village of Mousehole to visit the Post Office and Ms. Pengelly. It was just before nine a.m. on a typical British cloudy day. Showers were expected, but he decided to walk anyway. It was not that far, and he figured the exercise would be good for him.

The post office was back down the hill, left on Commercial and right on North Cliff. He remembered the traffic warden pointing it out as a landmark yesterday. He quickly found it, a small brick building on the narrow North Cliff Road. The sun was peeking through the cloudy morning sky, and he was happy to be there. The Post Office was not busy, and he found Ms. Pengelley behind the counter sorting papers. He had expected to see a skinny woman in her eighties with a knot of grey hair pulled back and round horn-rimmed glasses. To Robert's surprise and delight, he found a healthy woman in her early sixties with red cheeks that almost matched her red hair. Her hazel eyes twinkled as Robert asked if she was Ms. Pengelley.

She beamed at him. "And you are Robert!" "Yes!" he stood back, eyebrows raised.

"Peggy called me and told me you might be around with questions, trying to figure out your past." She smiled and radiated a welcome towards Robert. She opened the door between the building's side wall and the counter that separated them and almost threw herself in Robert's arms, giving him a big hug. "I was your teacher, you know, back then. I am so happy to see you and to know you are OK."

She invited Robert through the door and offered him a seat at a table behind the counter. It was half full of ink stamps, official-looking papers, and a cup of tea.

She was beaming and repeated herself, "I can't tell you how happy I am to see you. None of us knew what ever became of you after you left the hospital with your uncle." Her tone changed and became more solemn. "You know when your parents went missing?"

"What happened?" Robert asked.

"No one knows for sure. Some local fishermen discovered your parents floating in the ocean. There were also two other bodies in the water nearby, a man and a woman. They didn't have any identification, so we just cremated them. We buried your parents. It was very sad, but then the war went on. There was a big invasion in France. It started a few days after we found your parents. There were armies everywhere: British, American, Canadian, and French. The mystery of your parents slipped from the headlines as more news about others fighting in the war, well, you know, soldiers' bodies were sent home. It was war, and people died, and while we became accustomed to it, we have never forgotten them. And we certainly have not forgotten your parents. They were good folks, always ready to lend a hand and help others."

Robert felt his face flush as images of his parents' last moments filled his imagination. His emotions took over as tears ran down his cheeks. Taking the tissue Ms. Pengelly offered him, he said, "I am sorry, this is all so new to me. I have managed to forget ever living in Mousehole, and now I am here, memories are coming back, and I seem to veer between anger and sadness. I feel as if I am on an emotional roller coaster."

Ms. Pengelly was quick to reassure him. "I completely understand. To this day, a small group of us go to the churchyard in early spring and do some work around the gravestones. We take tea and sandwiches and sit for a while remembering all the people we lost. It usually ends with us weeping a little as we recount how it was back then. Our memories and stories we share, in some way, have kept them alive." She shrugged her head, "and we should never forget those who gave their lives. "But," and now she shifted her body as if to shrug off bad memories,

"I am so glad to see you, and I know Walt will be too!"

"Who is Walt?"

"Well! He was your best mate." "He was?"

"Yes, you were as thick as thieves. You and Walter Hammett were always getting each other in trouble." She was smiling, amused at the memory of the two scruffy boys with grimy hands and dirt on their knees.

Ms. Pengelley told him more about his childhood, his family, others in the small community, and his friend, Walter.

"He is still here, you know?"

Robert eagerly replied, "Really! So, I can get to see him?"

'Yes, he runs the chippy."

"What, the one in town, near the harbor?"

"Yes, that's the one. The High Tide"

"That's funny. I was there yesterday! He may have even served me!"

Still smiling, Ms. Pengelly said, "You could find him. I am sure you would have a lot to catch up on!'

The pictures in Robert's mind were taking shape and becoming defined. The mist was lifting, and it was as if a hand was reaching out to him on that dark precipice he had dreamed of, reaching out to save him.

People came and went, purchased stamps, posted letters, and asked questions. Ms. Pengelly introduced Robert to those she knew and quickly served those she did not. She promptly got back to Robert, recounting the past. It was around 11:30 a.m. Robert stood up and thanked Ms. Pengelley for all her help and for answering his questions. "Robert, the pleasure is mine," she told him, "I can't tell you how happy I am to see you, and I want to meet your family. Promise you will come back."

It was as if someone close had just placed a blanket

around his shoulders. Familiar, loving. He felt a lump in his throat. "I hope I can. I would love for you to meet them and for me to show them Muzzle and Penzance and where I grew up." As he approached the door, "Peggy asked me to remind you about a council meeting this evening."

She laughed. "Next time I see Peggy, I'll remind her I've never missed a meeting yet." She laughed again." Come back soon, Robert." as he left the post office and closed the door behind him

* * *

He returned to the hotel, got the rental car, and drove to Madron, a small town a few miles away, where his parents were buried. Ms. Pengelley had given him clear directions to the parish church and drew a map locating their grave.

The church was easy to find, and the ancient graveyard was tidy and well cared for. Robert sat on the ground staring at the inscription, 'In memory of Reggie and Florence Hall who were lost at Sea and now returned.' He was in the graveyard for about two hours. In his mind, he retraced the conversations with Peggy Mesa at the house where he lived as a child, Maria Dawson, the hospital administrator, and Margaret Pengelly, the Posty. There was a lot of information to sort through. His emotions were all over the place as he wiped tears from his cheeks and spoke to his dead parents. Out loud, he asked questions they would never answer, perhaps not even if they were alive.

He photographed and sketched the stone-built Norman Church and his parents' graves. It was a meditation of sorts and helped him gather the pieces of the jigsaw of faint memories, dreams, and what he had learned about the war.

A cold chill began to wrap itself around Robert. It brought him out of his reverie. Clouds were gathering, suggesting rain was imminent. He packed up his notepad and pencils, returned to the rental car, got in, and sat there while reflecting on what he had learned, pondering what had taken him from Mousehole, a little village not far from Penzance in Cornwall, England, to life in America.

Walter Hammet knows

That evening, Robert worked on his notes and drawings, adding bits and pieces of details shared with him over the last couple of days. By mid-morning the following day, he was ready to go and find Walter Hammet, his childhood friend.

The High Tide Chippy was down from the hotel and past the Post Office. He followed Chapel Street towards the Methodist Church and then left. Robert stopped in his tracks. Yesterday, his mind was full of other things, and he had not noticed that he was on Portland Place. Shrugging, he put his shoulders back and rolled his eyes as he opened his hands. He realized where he lived as a child and his home in the U.S. were connected. Portland Place, Mousehole, England, and Portland, Maine, USA. He was grinning.

He walked slowly past the little stone houses with flower boxes on the window ledges to the Chippy with a bench seat outside. It had a large glass door and small windows that, he figured, if local people were not determined to preserve the historic nature of this community, would have been replaced years ago with something more modern.

The glass door seemed to be out of place. Robert stood back, the Architect in him examining the structure, thinking the door was probably a concession made by the powers that be in this little town—a concession to progress which, as much as possible, they would slow down.

Looking through the glass door, Robert saw someone inside behind the large, shiny steel counter. There were just two tables inside, each with a couple of chairs. It was barely 11 a.m., and the sign on the door said, 'Open at 11: 30 a.m.'. He turned away and walked up the street, changed his mind, turned around, and returned. He tried the door handle.

A voice yelled out in what was to Robert's ears a strange accent. "Not open, mate, over fifteen minutes. Everything ain't ready yet."

Robert nodded and waved his hand as if to say okay. He walked away, stopped, turned, and walked back. He knocked on the door again, caught the man's attention, and beckoned him.

The man walked over, opened the door, and, in a somewhat irritated tone, asked, "What's up mate, we ain't ready yet, like I just said, why doncha just take a seat there." He pointed to the bench.

Robert replied, "Yes, I know, but I am Robert. You

know Robert Hall, you are Walter. Walter Hammett? We were friends as kids."

"Nah, not me, mate. I work *'ere*. I'm Peter. (It sounded like *Pea er*, with the t dropped). Walt is at the market this morning. I expect *im* back soon. Come back in a while. I'll tell *im* you were *ere*." Now, somewhat more conciliatory. "What's *yer* name again?"

Robert took a business card from his wallet, wrote the hotel number on the back, and handed it to Peter. (or *Pea er,* as he would say it)

"Come back around 12:30, mate. *e* will be *ere* then. I'll tell *im* to look out for you."

Robert decided to come back, thanked Peter for his help, and wandered off. He walked along the stony beach, bought some postcards, and then at 12:30, went back to the 'Chippy.' As he approached the front door, he could easily see two men inside behind the counter. They looked at Robert, then at each other, and then at Robert as he gingerly stepped over the threshold. Immediately, Walter came from behind the counter wearing head-to-toe white pants, shoes, a shirt, and an apron tied around the front. He was a burly man with a bit of a pot belly, clean-shaven with thinning grey hair. He had brown eyes and gnarly hands, one of which he cautiously offered to Robert.

There was uncertainty and some of that British reserve. But then, as he recognized Robert, he exclaimed, "Well, if it ain't Robby Hall, now you are a bloody sight for sore eyes if ever there were one! Where have you been hiding all these years?"

"I am sorry," Robert said, "is this a bad time?"

Walter reassured him. "No way, mate, I would not miss this for the world. I often wondered what happened to you, and look." holding both his gnarly hands open in front of him, "Here you are, after all these years."

They started to chat about their shared past, not that Robert could remember much of it, and as the chippy began to get busy with the lunchtime rush, they agreed to have a drink at the pub that evening.

They both smiled, stood up, and shook hands. Walter took Robert's hand with both hands, "See you later at the Kings Arms in Paul. It is the next village, up Muzzle Lane, past the school.

You remember where that is?"

Robert hesitated, "Err, no, not really, but I will find it." "Well, OK, but if you leave from your hotel, it's a few minutes' drive and only about a fifteen-minute walk."

Robert left the Chippy and retraced his steps up Portland Place, his mind and gut in turmoil. He felt elated, nervous, unsure, and even a bit scared. He was also excited, anticipating what else he may discover about his life here in Mousehole, where time seemed to have almost stood still, a place that used to be his home.

* * *

Robert returned to his hotel, went to his room, got his notebook from the shelf above the bed, sat in the leather chair, and made notes about his conversations that day.

While reflecting on his conversation with Margaret Pengelley, he remembered her now. He drew a picture of her standing at the chalkboard in the classroom as he remembered her then, a different person but still with that same smile, an infectious sense of fun and joy about her.

Robert got lost in his sketch. He drew a few lines, stopped, and remembered being with Walt on an adventure to the beach and having breakfast with his parents. Memories long buried in his subconscious were resurfacing. He had trouble keeping up with them, but he could now recall how his parents smelled and the sound of their voices. Images of where he lived as a child sprung to Robert's mind. He remembered the cozy feeling in the kitchen as he ate breakfast, sitting on a small chair next to the wood stove in the house now owned by Peggy Mesa.

Time passed unnoticed as his mind allowed his hands

to do the work, then returning to the here and now, the sketch was almost done. He had become so lost and caught up with the images of his past that he had little memory of doing it. He looked as if surprised at how nearly complete it was. He made a few notes on the notepad, then looked at his watch. It was 7:30, and it was time to go to the pub and all its temptations. The King's Arms in the village of Paul was a low-rise building with vines creeping over doors and around windows. Robert, somewhat hesitatingly, entered and found himself in a cozy, warm, welcoming Pub with its low ceiling and exposed beams that had weathered two hundred years of people coming and going; regulars and strangers were all welcome. A small group of five people stood at the bar, laughing. Others were seated at little round tables and a few booths big enough for six. Robert looked around. Walt saw him standing at the entrance looking lost and waved to him. Robert acknowledged him with a nod, walked to the table, removed his jacket, and slid into the booth bench seat across from Walt.

They talked about family, other friends, and mischief as children. They recounted shared experiences: getting into trouble for stealing apples, the war, and their day trips to St Michael's Mount, which was just a fifteen-minute ride on their bikes and where they would play in coves and search the beaches for treasures while making sure to be home for tea.

More memories were released from the jaws of the past trauma. Robert searched Walt's memory with more questions, looking for details and imagining what it was like for him back then. Things were falling into place. Two and half hours slipped by as the two men recalled their early childhood together.

"Remember that fight?" Walt said. "Some other kids were taking the piss out of my name. You know the same as always, Hammy Hammett. You must be a pig, piggy Walt. They teased me endlessly until, one day, I had enough. Luckily, you were there. It was four against one, but you evened it up, remember?" "No, I don't, but then there is a lot I don't remember. Did we win?"

Walter grinned, "Mate, I must tell you, when you got angry, you seemed to lose it, and we gave those kids a run for their money! I got a black eye, and you got a ripped shirt, but they never bothered me again!"

Over a couple of typically British pints of ale for Walt and diet coke with lemon for Robert, they probed the past and explored what was remembered, imagined, and forgotten. Robert succumbed again to the promise of shepherd's pie. He finished his dinner and said, "That was much better than a couple of nights ago,"

"Yes, well," Walt replied, you have to choose the right place!"

They talked about his problems with alcohol, his kids, Henry disappearing, and the remaining mystery of why Henry was going to Canada on a snow-swept night when he said he was going to Boston. Robert was honest with Walt and opened up about his life.

"My marriage is in trouble because of the booze. I can't blame Caroline, of course. With her dad and everything, I am determined to make it right. This trip, which I should have done long ago, has unlocked a lot of memories, and I know I am done with drinking. No more hiding the pain and sadness."

Walt, for his part, was a good listener and shared some of his innermost thoughts. He was married once. "It never worked out," he told Robert. "Now, there is a woman in town, Dorothy, Dot. She lives in Penzance, and she was married and now divorced with two teenage girls. We see each other a couple of times a week and at weekends. Maybe you will meet her if you stick around for a few days."

"I must leave on Wednesday and still need to do some things. It'll be Thursday when I get back. But thanks. My next trip will, hopefully, be with my family, and then we can take some more time to tell stories of our past. It's been stressful, but I think I can get back on track with Caroline. At least, I am hoping."

The evening evaporated as if it were just a few minutes, and then it was over. It was time to go. They stood outside the pub.

"Did you drive Robbie?"

Walt had now switched to calling him by the name he knew him as when they were kids.

Robert laughed. "That's funny. I've never been called Robbie.

I wouldn't allow it, but it sounds okay coming from you!"

"Well, that's what you were back then!" Both men gave a slight shrug of their shoulders, and Robert answered, "I left the car and walked."

"I can give you a ride?"

"No," while patting his stomach. "I'll walk. I could do with the exercise!"

"Next time you should stay with me, at my house. I live here in Paul, and you would be welcome."

"Thank you, and thanks for this evening and everything. It means a lot to me, more than I can say. So many years of my life have been a mystery, and now it looks like I finally have answers." He fought back a sad feeling that, if he allowed it, would have seen him in tears.

They said goodbye and, this time, hugged—a manly hug, not too long, just enough to say more than a handshake would.

Robert left the lights of the pub and the surrounding few houses behind him and walked into the darkness. The sky was full of stars and a waning half-moon. His eyes adjusted, and he could see the red glow of Penzance on the dark horizon ahead of him. He walked past a small farm with recently plowed fields, an earthy smell drifting in the night air. A large tractor tire was leaning on a low stone wall beside the farm gate. He stopped, hauled himself on it, and thought about how Walt called him Robbie. A chill ran down his spine. He was alone but, at that point, not lonely.

He looked at the sky and talked aloud, thinking of his parents. "What happened to you? Why were you killed? Who left your bodies floating in the ocean?" He gave in to his feelings, and tears rolled down his cheeks.

Before driving back to Heathrow Airport and catching his flight back to America, he wandered the surrounding villages and the secret coves not far from the house he had lived in.

Assuring them, and more importantly, himself, he

would return with his family, he met again with and said goodbye to Peggy Messa, Margaret Pengelley, and Walter Hammett, the people who had known more about him as a child than he knew about himself.

Meeting Mom and Dad

Portland Maine 1955

Being in love is exotic. The world's colors are brighter and sharper. Enjoying a particular song together is special, and inexpensive food at a small, romantic restaurant is perfect. A smile or a touch can bring shivers down your spine. You inhabit a world swirling with all the possibilities that life holds out in front of you. Then you announce to family and friends that you want to be with this person forever, till death do us part.

But for Robert and Caroline, that time had not yet arrived. They had not admitted to each other or themselves that they were in love. For now, they were young students driving from Boston to Portland, Maine, for a family Sunday lunch.

Delores Stern, Caroline's Mother, had not yet succumbed to the cancer she had been fighting for years. It was in remission, and she looked forward to meeting this young man Caroline had been telling her about.

Delores looked at her watch. It was 11:30. They were

expected in half an hour. All morning, she had been issuing orders to Maggie, her long-time housekeeper. Maggie would shop, make beds, clean, cook light meals, and generally be an extension of Delores's hands around the house. When Delores was off at various charity board meetings, Maggie would be there to keep an eye on things. She had worked for Henry and Delores for many years and been with them through good and bad times. She was discreet and knew not to talk about the family. Maggie would oversee the caterers if they entertained on a grand scale, but this was an informal family lunch. Maggie would return to her family once lunch was prepared.

Everyone was curious about this person Caroline was bringing home, and none more than Henry. "What do you think this means? Are they serious?" he asked Delores that morning over breakfast. "And what do you know about him?"

"He is studying to be an architect and lives with an uncle when he is not on Campus. He is, or was, British but moved here as a child, and that's about all I know."

"Well, it's not much to go on," Henry grumbled. "She must have told you more. What are you keeping from me? Are they sleeping together?"

"That's enough, Henry. Your daughter is a grown woman, and I don't even want to think about it!"

Henry mumbled, "Well, I still pay the bills. To me, she is still a child."

Caroline had boyfriends and dated at High School but never brought anyone home for Sunday lunch to meet her parents!

Delores looked over her glasses and said, "Not another word!" She had talked to Robert a little about her parents but not any details, and while she tried to reassure him, it did not help. He was on edge, especially about meeting Henry. Knowing her dad's dark side, Caroline was just a little nervous about how Henry would be with Robert.

Henry Stern was difficult to get to know, and he never really shared his deepest feelings and anxieties with anyone, including his wife. He was sometimes outgoing and gregarious, but even though he tried to hide his dark side, he could be broody at other times. The only person he would confide in was David Preston.

They shared secrets and unquestionably trusted each other. Some things could only be discussed with David and remained just between them. They rarely, if ever, talked about what bound them together. Henry's wife also never got to hear those stories; Caroline was less concerned about her mother, who she knew was looking forward to meeting Robert.

In a phone conversation, Delores invited and encouraged her to bring Robert for lunch and told her, "Now, don't worry about your dad, Caroline. I will take care of that, and if Robert is as you say he is, then he is more than welcome."

David Preston and Jenny McCarthy, Henry's secretary, and her husband and two children were also invited. Caroline and Robert arrived just as Maggie was leaving, and she welcomed Caroline with a hug and shook Robert's hand.

"Welcome, so nice to meet you. How was the drive?" Robert nodded his head. "How is school, Caroline?"

She also responded with a nod and added, "Oh, you know, work-work-work, but OK, I am enjoying it."

They smiled and hugged again, and Maggie left for the rest of the day. As Maggie left, Henry and Delores came from the kitchen. There were big smiles all around. "Welcome, so nice to meet you. How was the drive? How is school?" Henry asked as he hugged Caroline and offered his hand to Robert. They shook, and Henry held onto Robert's hand just a bit longer than necessary, causing Robert immediate discomfort. It was a subtle form of dominance and control.

He looked him straight in the eye as he welcomed him, sizing him up. "So, you are the Robert we have heard so much about!" Robert smiled, "I hope so!" he said as he retrieved his hand.

Lunch in the garden overlooking Casco Bay was relaxed and very pleasant. Jenny McCarthy's two children could hardly wait to leave the table and play ball in the garden. Her husband helped Caroline and Delores clear dishes while Jenny joined her two kids, leaving David with Henry and Robert.

"Come with me," Henry told Robert, "I want to show you something." And turning to David, "You, OK?" David nodded just slightly and poured himself more wine. "I'm good. I'll wait here for dessert." He suspected their conversation was to be a little private.

Typical Henry, find out more about who you are dealing with.

Robert followed Henry as they headed to the little stone wall that defined the property boundary from the sandy beach. They stepped over the stone wall and sat on it, in silence at first, watching the sailboats bobbing along in the afternoon breeze.

"Do you like to sail, Robert?"

"I do. As a teenager, we used to sail Lasers at a club in Boston, on the Charles River."

"We?" Henry asked.

"My Uncle William, Bill. I have lived with him and my Aunt Nancy for as long as I can remember. Mom and Dad died in the war in Europe, and I don't remember anything about them. My uncle never talks about it, and Nancy, my aunt, is American and was never in Europe. I plan on going back there one day to find my roots. I only know that I lived in Southwest Cornwall before I was ten, somewhere in a small village overlooking the English Channel. My Dad was a fisherman, and my mom worked at home. They had a small farm where they grew vegetables, and Dad would sell some at the market."

Henry watched Robert as he spoke, sizing him up and wondering if he would see more of this young man. Although you would not know it to look at him, Henry's stomach churned as Robert talked. Images he had chased from his mind dropped over him and briefly engulfed him. For a moment, he was transported back to a time he wished he had never experienced.

"You mean you don't remember anything about your childhood? The village, your school, your house, or your parents?"

"It's all a bit vague, and Uncle Bill doesn't know what happened to my mom and Dad. They sort of just disappeared. It was the war. That's about all I know. It's like a whole part of me I don't understand. It can be a bit frustrating sometimes. My life before then is pretty much a blank. Uncle Bill never wants to discuss it. He insists that I have all the information and changes the subject. Don't get me wrong. I love America. It is my home. But I plan to return to Europe someday to see if I can find any trace of my parents."

They talked a little more about what Robert did know, and as they did, Henry became increasingly uncomfortable.

"I was in Europe during the war,"

Henry said. "Logistics, Transport." Henry then returned to a dark place in his mind and stared out in the distance, across the water. There was one of those awkward silences, and then turning to Robert, "So, why architecture?" And without waiting for an answer,

"Maybe you will build something for me one day."

"You never know," Robert said as Caroline popped over the little stone wall.

"Is he interrogating you, Robert?"

"I was about to interrogate him right back," was

Robert's quick response.

And with that, Caroline took his hand, looked at her dad, and with a smile, "Juries out, Dad, let's get dessert!" All three smiled as they returned for coffee and dessert at the lunch table.

The afternoon passed, and it was time for everyone to say their goodbyes. Robert thanked Delores and Henry for a perfect afternoon. Caroline hugged her parents. Robert shook Henry's hand and then extended his hand to Delores. She pushed it to one side, briefly hugged him, gave him a peck on the cheek, and said, "Come back again, Robert. You are most welcome."

Once in the car with Robert, heading towards Rte. 95, Caroline said, "Well, you certainly won my mom over, you charmer!"

Robert smiled. "She was very welcoming to me."

Caroline asked, "So what did you and Dad talk about?"

"Nothing much," Robert said as he rested his hand on Caroline's knee. "He wanted to know about my family, where I was born, that sort of thing."

"What did you tell him?"

"Not much to tell. I live in Boston with my uncle, and that's all. He was also curious to know about my plans for the future."

"He would!" Caroline smiled. "He's always concerned about me and wants me to join the business when I get ready."

"Is that something you want to do?"

"Probably, unless you whisk me away to some island paradise and keep me barefoot and pregnant."

The mood was light. They both laughed again as Robert turned the car onto the Rte. 95 ramp and headed for Boston.

Over the next eighteen months, Robert and Caroline grew closer and eventually announced their intention to marry and have many kids.

* * *

Henry was on a mission. At Caroline's engagement party on a summer's day on the lawn of his house, he ensured he had a private conversation with Uncle William. Henry wanted to know more about William and his soon-to-be son-in-law's past. Steering William away from everyone, they chatted over a glass of champagne, which Henry never really cared for; he would prefer a scotch.

They talked about the war, where they served, and in what capacity. Henry had suspicions and was probing around, asking questions, and trying to establish whether a connection to his and David's past was possible. His line of conversation seemed innocent enough, just the kind of thing people do in a social situation when meeting new people, looking for common ground and connection. Long buried images from back then floated into Henry's mind as they chatted, hanging over him, threatening. He took a long look at William Hall. He reminded him of someone he once knew, but he pushed the idea deep down into a corner of his mind, into a room without a window or light. He could not allow those memories to take control.

Just one week after the engagement party, Henry heard from Robert's uncle. It had been a difficult week. He had returned home from meetings in New York late Friday evening and awoke late on Saturday morning. Unshaven, he was barefoot, in sweatpants and an old sweater, as he went from the kitchen to his den. Delores had left some mail for him on his desk. He looked through them, singling out one that gave him pause.

Sitting in the overstuffed chair to the side of the desk, Henry opened the letter, a handwritten note thanking him:

"Dear Henry, it was a pleasure to meet you. Thank you so much for being a kind host and for your generosity in welcoming my nephew to your family. We had little time to talk at the party, and I think we have some things to discuss.

As you know, I left Cornwall towards the war's end, and I think we may have met once or twice. You were in a pub with my brother. You and I may have a few shared experiences and secrets. But I am guessing you probably want them to remain secret. Let me know the next time you are in Boston. We can have dinner perhaps, or if pushed for time, maybe just a drink.

Sincerely,

William Hall"

Henry sat looking at the note in silence. There was a knot in his gut. He screwed the paper into a ball and tossed it onto the desk, and sat looking at it. Quietly, he said, "I don't believe this is possible."

After a few minutes, he got up, unfurled the paper, picked up the phone on his desk, and dialed the number. It rang three times, four, five, six rings, and as he was about to hang up, there was an answer.

"Hello, this is William."

"Good morning, William," Henry said in a low voice. He was careful not to be heard by his wife, currently just outside his den hanging a large, framed photo of Robert and Caroline in the hallway, along with other pictures in the 'Rouges Gallery' as Henry called it.

"This is Henry Stern."

A cheery voice answered back. "Good morning, Henry. How are you today?"

"What do you want?" Henry asked.

"What do you mean? Why would I want anything from you?" sarcastically, "It's not as if you could replace anything I have lost in my life, right?"

Henry, still talking in a hushed voice, "You know what I mean. It did not take you long to figure it out, and now I guess there is something you want?"

"Well, maybe you can help me a bit," William said, "but I don't think we should discuss this now, not over the phone. We can be helpful to each other. It's not as if I want to upset Caroline or ruin her life and love, but I think we can do something for each other."

"There is nothing you can do for me," Henry said.

"Oh, I think there may be Henry. I could keep my secrets to myself, you know, let sleeping dogs die," he paused, "err, lie."

Henry agreed to meet. "I will be in Boston on Tuesday at the Copley Plaza. Meet me in the hotel bar at 6 p.m." Then he hung up.

Henry sat for a few minutes, his brain grinding out a series of possibilities.

He went upstairs, showered, dressed, and headed

downstairs again, stopping at the rogues' gallery to admire the newly framed photo. He entered the kitchen, looking for Delores. She sat at the kitchen island with her coffee and the morning newspaper. "The photos look good out there," he said, adding,

"We had better keep enough room for the grandchildren!" He smiled as he kissed Delores on the cheek.

"I do hope so," she returned his kiss. "I will be back in a couple of hours. I have paperwork to attend to."

He went to his office, where he called David Preston as soon as he arrived.

"You met Robert's uncle last week at the party.

Did you have much of a chance to talk to him?"

"No, I didn't. Why?"

"No conversation about England before he came to America?"

"No," and sensing the strain in Henry's voice.

"Why, what's this about? Why do you ask?"

Henry said, "He knows things from back then, in England. I am unsure what he knows, but I will meet him in Boston on Tuesday for a drink at the Copley."

"Henry, I don't like the sound of this. We have a lot at stake, and it may be best to stay away."

"I can't do that, David. Robert will become part of the family, and unfortunately, that means his uncle comes as part of the package. I don't fucking believe this. I hope I am wrong, but he will ask me for money."

"Why do you say that?"

"It's his tone. We shared background stories, you know, about the war, but I was discreet and did not say very much about, you know, you know what I am talking about, David."

David said, "How could that be possible?

Are you sure?"

Henry insisted. "He said things that were just a bit too close for comfort. I don't know what he thinks he knows or what he knows, but I am going to have to deal with it."

"Take it easy there, Henry. Let's get more information and see where it leads. I must attend a town hall meeting on Tuesday. But I can send someone to sit in the bar. You never know if you may need some help."

"Not sure that is necessary, but it may not be a bad idea."

"OK, I will arrange it. You will recognize the guy from other projects, and I suggest you don't talk to him; give him a slight nod to acknowledge him discreetly. David added, "Henry, let's stay calm and not let things go anywhere they shouldn't."

"Okay, I will give you a call on Wednesday."

The meeting on Tuesday came and went, as Henry had expected. William wanted money in return for remaining quiet about what he knew. The past would stay in the past. He would keep what he knew about Henry and David secret. Robert's Uncle Bill would move to California or Hawaii after the wedding, which would be the end of it. It was a promise that Henry doubted would be kept.

* * *

Three weeks later, Robert's Uncle Bill was buried. He died suddenly, the victim of a hit-and-run accident in Quincy, south of Boston. The Police found the car crashed into a wall on a side street. The driver was nowhere to be seen. Henry and David, old friends with a history going back many years, had resolved the problem.

The news of his uncle's sudden death shook Robert. Understandably, he took it badly. Losing Uncle Bill was devastating to him and his Aunt Nancy. Robert was consoled by the love and warmth he received from Caroline's family, especially Henry. Robert felt secure in his welcome to the family. Robert's aunt eventually moved back to California, where she had grown up. Robert's ties to England and his past were now buried with his uncle. His closest family now was his soon-to-be new wife and her family.

Sometimes, when we are young, we do foolish things. When we are young, we are invincible. The world is in front of us, and everything is possible. If lucky, most of us will escape our youth unscathed. Young men sometimes make bad decisions that can haunt them for the rest of their lives.

Carrying those ghosts of the past can be daunting. Sadly, when the secrets of the past catch up, people's lives can be ruined.

What To Do

Portland Maine 1974

The following morning, having completed the report to the Police as promised, Caroline walked the few blocks from the station house to Em's apartment. She crossed Commercial Street and entered the lobby of a recently completed conversion of old warehouses.

She pushed the doorbell; Em buzzed her in. Caroline entered, took the elevator to the fourth floor, and opened the door to Ems's apartment.

"Hi, anyone home," she called as she entered.

"In the kitchen, coffee is brewing."

Caroline removed her coat, put it on the hook near the door, kicked her shoes off, and entered the open-plan living room, kitchen, and dining room. A black cat with strands of white on his face rubbed against her leg. Caroline picked her up, kissed her, "Hi, there, Popcorn," and carried her to the kitchen. She put the cat on the floor and sat on the stool on the kitchen island.

"Em, it's spooky. The police know more than they

are telling me. They say it's an ongoing investigation into war crimes, and somehow my dad and Uncle David are, were", she corrected herself, "Involved."

"What's going to happen now?" asked Em as she poured the coffee and slid a cup across the kitchen island counter to Caroline.

"I don't know. The police told me to go home and said they would call me and let me know if they needed to talk again."

"Did you manage to speak with the woman at the Hotel? What was it?"

"The Borderline. No, they told me not to. Said they would be talking to her, and I should not call her."

"So, it's all a blank?" Em asked.

Caroline sipped her coffee and said, "I don't know. I am worried. They did say that my dad was involved, and they are not sure until they speak more with Frank Lee."

Em said, "They have to catch him first."

Caroline replied, "They picked him up at the toll booth on 95 last night. He was heading to Canada, and they had him somewhere in Portland."

Em interrupted, "Finally, perhaps now you can get some answers."

"Well, yes, but what if Dad was involved in

something, even if it was long ago? They said that if he was, and it was possible, they could keep his name out of it. And in any case, they would let me know before they did anything. They also plan to talk to David Preston when he returns from his trip."

Em picked up her coffee, lifted her chin, and pointed her nose to the couches. "Let's go and sit over there," she said.

Popcorn followed Caroline and jumped onto the couch beside her, stretched out on its back, bathing in a sliver of sunlight piercing through the window. Caroline reached out and scratched her belly.

Em asked, "Are they going to talk to David? When is he due back?"

"I think later this evening. It's scary. Part of me wishes Robert were here. I haven't heard from him. He left several messages on the answering machine, but I couldn't call him. He is due back the day after tomorrow, I think. Anyway, the kids will be home from ski camp at the weekend."

"What's going to happen To Robert?"

"For now, he'll continue to stay at the Hotel. I feel so confused and miss him, but, well, you know."

"Well, I am not sure I do. Men and me, you know

how that is!"

Caroline nodded her head and agreed as Em continued. "David must know something. He was with your dad during the war. I know. It's hard to believe, but I think it is a possibility.

"Yes, but what? What could he possibly be involved in?" then answering her own question, "Not Nazis, of that I can be sure! The police said they would speak to David in due course, but they seemed casual about it. Sergeant Hope told me not to worry, and they would have an informal talk with him when he returned from the trade mission."

"What's going to happen to Frank Lee?"

"He is, apparently, possibly, a war criminal. Can you believe that?" Not waiting for an answer, "They said when they were finished questioning him, he would eventually be sent back to Germany for trial."

"I knew that story yesterday, when he burst in on you at Henry's house, was a crock."

Caroline was nodding in agreement.

"And the woman, Claire, at the Borderline Hotel in Canada, what about her?" EM asked.

"Well, as I said, I don't know anything yet. Somehow, she is involved, but I have no idea in what way. I hope she was just my dad's lover, which would be best. But

I must wait till the police have spoken to her."

Em was smiling.

"What so funny?" Asked Caroline.

"Henry with a lover, and you don't care, very open-minded of you! Next thing I know, you will be burning your bra! Gloria Steinman would be proud of you, Caroline!"

They both laughed. Caroline got up, walked to the door, and retrieved her coat and boots. She then turned to Em. "I have decided to sell the company. I think it's for the best. If Dad were involved with Frank Lee, that would take him out of the spotlight. Honestly, it's more than I want to handle now."

"Oh," said Em as she picked up Popcorn. She had followed them to the door. "Does that mean I will no longer be able to refer to you as my rich and powerful friend?" And then smiling, "Just rich!"

Caroline laughed, scratched Popcorn's head, and said, "Just a good friend, Em, the best. That's plenty enough for me."

She kissed Em on the cheek and left.

* * *

David Preston arrived at Boston Logan Airport that afternoon. He got through the usual airport formalities and called a number he had committed to memory before he collected his bag.

"It's me. Did it get done?"

"No." the voice on the other end of the line said. "The police picked him up yesterday."

"What! Why not? What happened?"

"I finally tracked him down near where he keeps his shitty hot dog wagon in Boston. Luckily, I did because he was heading to Portland. I followed, thinking he was heading to Canada and looking for an opportunity to grab him when nobody could spot what was happening. Then he left 95 at Portland and went to Henry's house."

"What?"

"He was there for a while. Caroline's car was in the driveway. He hurriedly left, and I followed him back onto 95 North. I guessed that he was going to Canada after all. I figured I could get him to stop on the highway alone, but the police pulled him over at the toll booth."

"Fuck!" David slammed the phone down. He stood there for a while, and he then called Caroline.

"Hi Caroline, I just arrived in Boston and will be in Portland tomorrow. How about we catch up? We can get some lunch together, perhaps?"

Caroline interrupted him and explained her decision to sell and move on. "Well, that certainly gives us a lot to talk about. I will be there around noon. Yes, good. Have you heard from Robert?

Caroline explained that they keep missing each other because of the time differences between the U.S. and the U.K. and when she expects him to return.

"Okay, good enough, Caroline, I'll see you tomorrow, bye."

Feeling queasy, he put the phone down and quickly found a bathroom. While washing his hands, it was all he could do to control his anger. He looked in the mirror and said to his reflection, "You are so screwed. Fuck this, and fuck you, Henry, for dying like that."

He then told his reflection, "Be very careful. Everything you have worked for could be destroyed, and you will be ruined."

Desperation

Paris, France. 1942

Paris was not a good place to be in 1942. The German military cooperated with the Gestapo, and the Vichy government helped them. Everyone, including the police and militia, had to cooperate, a condition of the Armistice. The French Militia helped the Gestapo head, Klaus Barbie, to arrest members of the resistance, minorities, and Jews for shipment to the Drancy Deportation Camp in Northeast Paris and to Auschwitz, Dachau, and Buchenwald concentration camps. People went underground to avoid imprisonment and inevitable death, and many defected or joined the resistance.

Secrets in German-occupied Paris were hard to keep, becoming currency to the scared and the ruthless. People would share what they knew to survive for another month, a week, or even a day.

Gerhard Moller, a Nazi officer stationed in Paris, was convinced Germany would be defeated and decided that for his future good health, he should get away from Europe to somewhere safe. He had no idea what to do until, by chance, he met Bette Caron.

Bette Caron was French, a mid-level analyst for the Vichy Government who was spying for the Allies. She would read reports and study data to identify Jews who would be arrested and taken to Drancy. Bette Caron knew about escape routes from France to the UK, mainly for British and Americans shot down behind enemy lines. Once she had a workable plan, she would need to contact the right people and prepare paperwork. Having helped many embark on dangerous journeys away from the war, and could see no reason not to help herself. She hated her life. Her contacts, the allies, refused to allow her to leave her job. Women who could blend in and were smart could be an excellent information resource. They insisted she would be most valuable to the war effort if she stayed working for the Vichy Government. She decided to take matters into her own hands.

A Jewish couple, Claire and Francois Leblanc, also planned to escape the madness and make a new life together. Unknown to them, Bette Caron, who had seen their names on a list of people to be rounded up and sent to Drancy, had been observing them. Bette soon became obsessed with using their identities to travel and escape to America. With the correct paperwork, sometimes posing as French Jews and at other times as a French Jew with a German guard seemed to have the best chance of success. She needed help, a partner, and a German who knew how to fight if a situation arose. She met Gerhard Moller by chance through her work for the Government, and he seemed to fit the requirement, disillusioned and scared, and a German officer who could get them through some of the more treacherous checkpoints.

One evening in a bar in a Paris suburb, Bette Caron and Gerhard Moller met as planned. And as dangerous as it was to share her plan, she had to trust him. Over drinks, lightheartedly, as if it was just theory. They speculated about how to escape. Finally, Bette Caron shared what she had in mind.

* * *

In 1940 when the Nazis took over France, Galleries Lafayette had been serving the public since 1893 on the corner of Rue La Fayette and Rue de la Chaussée d'Antin. Over the years, the Jewish owner, Théophile Bader, had annexed adjacent buildings and created a unique emporium. Bader had, by 1942, been forced to sell the business to non-Jews and was eventually arrested and hauled off to a concentration camp, where he died. His cousins Claire Leblanc and her husband Francois lived on the Vieille du Temple. in the fourth district of Paris. It was the Jewish

Quarter, the Marais. They were artisans and made necklaces, rings, brooches, and upmarket diamond engagement and wedding rings. They had been suppliers to Galleries Lafayette and feared it would not be long before they, along with others in the Jewish quarter, would follow the same destiny as their distant cousin. That is unless they did something to save themselves.

There was a constant threat, especially for Jews, of being arrested and hauled off to die somewhere in a brutal manner. Food prices had quadrupled and rationed. The black market thrived. While these were dangerous times, there were opportunities for those with their wits about them. The Leblancs were resourceful and could take advantage of the situation. As bad as their choices were, one that appeared open to them seemed the least dangerous option. They had the means and sufficient cash and diamonds to secure their journey, first to England and then to America. Unfortunately for them, there had been low-level gossip in the Marias about a small group of Jews planning an escape. Bette was always looking for information and had overheard the whispers. She found their names on the list of people soon to be arrested and transported to Drancy and put things together; they would be her way out. Bette knew the Leblancs were due to die anyway, so she thought, what difference does it matter where? In desperate times, people do desperate things.

The day before, the Leblancs would be arrested and taken to Drancy. Bette Caron and Officer Gerhard Moller went to Claire and Francoise Leblanc's apartment. They knew there was an escape route, but that was all, and it was a tightly guarded secret. They planned to persuade the LeBlancs that they should travel together. Then, posing as part of the resistance, they told them they would take them to a safe house away from the Jewish Quarter. They had speculated that if the couple chose to believe them and took the escape plan offered, there would be opportunities to 'lose' them during the journey if they felt it was necessary for their own survival.

* * *

Gerhard Moller and Bette Caron climbed the winding staircase to the third floor of the generally clean and tidy apartment building. Reaching the second floor, behind one door, they could hear a child cry; behind another, a man shouted, and from elsewhere, a violin playing a sad refrain. They knocked gently on the door to apartment 3. They knocked a second time before a woman in a head scarf and house coat carefully and partially opened the door. Just enough to see who was there.

Bette Caron said, "It's urgent. We must get you away

very soon. Your name is on the list, and they will be here tomorrow. It would be best if you left now. There is not much time, hurry!"

The woman, Clair Leblanc, was alarmed, "Quickly." She said, "Come in."

They entered the apartment, which had floor-to-ceiling windows, built-in bookcases, and, in one corner, two workstations where the couple worked and made jewelry for their primary client, Galleries Lafayette.

As soon as they stepped over the threshold and were inside, Francois Leblanc pointed a gun at them. "Stand there against the door, and don't move," he demanded. "Who are you? Why are you here?"

Bette Caron was ready with her story about being with the resistance. "We were sent to help you get away this evening and take what you need for the journey. We need to leave immediately. Hurry up. We need to go now!

Francois Leblanc did not believe them, and for the next fifteen minutes, Bette Caron and Gerhardt Moller were held at gunpoint and questioned. Then impatience and temper got the better of Gerhardt Moller, and the plan suddenly changed. He rushed Francois and grabbed the gun in a fit of impatience and anger. At the same time, Bette Caron rushed Claire and punched her in the face. As Claire doubled over, holding her face in pain, Bette Caron got behind her and held her with a knife at her throat. While hoping for compliance, the possibility of resistance had been expected and planned for.

Bette Caron had scant details of the plan and demanded to know from Francois, "Who are you going to meet? Are passwords needed to confirm who you are? How much money did you agree to pay? What time? Where?" All the while pushing the knife harder on Clair's neck.

At first, Claire and Francois resisted, and neither would answer. Gerhard Moller hit Francois across the face with the butt of the gun, and he collapsed on the floor. He then pulled a knife from his belt, turned from the crumpled body of Francois, and held it to Clair Leblanc's heart. Bette Caron still held Claire as Francois got off the floor and rushed Gerhard, who saw him coming and turned, pushing the knife into Francois. He fell to the floor and died. His wife screamed, "No, don't, I will tell you." But it was too late to save her husband.

Bette Caron was shaking and said, "It's your own fault. You should have told us. Now, we will come with you on the boat."

Clair pleaded, "Please, no. They are expecting only two, and you killed him. What will happen?" She sobbed uncontrollably, crouched on her knees, holding her dead husband, with his blood spattered on her hands, face, and clothes.

Bette Caron said, "If you want to stay alive, you will tell us what we need to know, and we will convince them to take us all. Like you, we want to get away." Claire was holding the body of her dead husband, body shaking, and tears rolling down her cheeks. Bette Caron tried to calm her down, "We did not want this, and we did not expect it to come to this. It's your fault; you should have cooperated."

Claire now felt so lost and alone. Her hopes for a future evaporated in a pool of her husband's blood. She told them what they wanted to know but lied about the money agreed for transport to England—pointing to a picture on the wall. "Behind the picture, there is a canvas bag. It is all for the captain when we get to the boat. Everything else is paid for."

Gerhard Moller then pushed Claire away from her Husband and kicked her in the stomach. Claire gasped as he sat across her body, put his hand around her throat, and strangled her.

Bette Caron stood back, shocked, stunned, and wide-eyed as Claire struggled and finally fell silent. She could do nothing to stop it, even if she wanted to. The Nazi Guard was trained to be a killer, and the murder was quick and efficient.

Moller and Caron ransacked the apartment. They retrieved the canvas bag from a hole in the wall behind the picture and scooped up other stones, strips of gold from the workbench, and an envelope with a handful of diamonds. They took what they needed. They put the bodies in the bed, covered them, and quietly left the building.

Two days later, Bette Caron and Gerhardt Moller became Claire and Francoise Leblanc, jewelry makers from the Marais, desperate to escape France and the Germans.

The Crossing

Le Quanqet, France, 1942

The journey to Le Quanqet was dangerous, and those trying to get out of France would rely on a network of British spies and French resistance fighters. Bette Carron had created forged papers, and Gerhard Moller had his officer's uniform to change into as needed. Mostly, they used their stolen identities; sometimes Bette posed as a prisoner, and other times as an Attachet of the German officer accompanying her. The Journey took six days using transport provided by the Resistance and British spies. They slept in forests and farm sheds, rested in safe houses, and took trains when they were considered safe.

It was a dangerous journey. Everyone, the British, French Underground, Germans, and Collaborators, were all their enemies. If found out, no doubt they would have been executed.

It was just a few days before the beginning of Operation Overlord, an American operation intended to invade the mainland and free Paris from the Germans. With their assumed identity of Claire and Francois Leblanc, Bette Carron and Gerhard Moller made their way to the pre-arranged dock and met with the captain and two other Jewish passengers, who were also escaping the Nazis. Under cover of darkness, with water up to their knees, they moved silently out into the water. They climbed into a small boat and rowed to a larger fishing boat. Pulling the rowboat over the stern of the larger vessel, they secured it and waited till morning. If they moved at night, there would be a good chance the German Marine Patrol would board them.

Fishermen were encouraged to work and help deal with the food shortages, which were a fact of life for the general population. Families who worked the fishing grounds for centuries were, ostensibly, under the protection of the German Navy. So, with luck, they would be ignored once this next stage of their journey began.

Nobody said much of anything; they just exchanged paperwork and money with the captain and found a place to sit in the fishing boat's uncomfortable and smelly cabin. They each ate some food taken from their bags and waited. In the pre-dawn light, the three men moved up on deck, and the two women stayed below, hiding from sight.

The men got the fishing boat ready. The captain started the engine as other small fishing boats in the harbor began to move out to the fishing grounds. "OK, let's go." the captain nodded to the two men at the front of the boat. The mooring lines splashed as they dropped into the water, and slowly, the boat moved towards the open sea, appearing as nothing more than three fishermen going to work.

The journey to the Cornish Coast was less than 100 miles. The boat could make 15 knots at top speed and cruise at 10. If they went directly, the journey time would be between 7 to ten hours. However, for the first 50 miles, they had to look like just another fishing boat, appearing to be working like any other vessel. They were expected to arrive on the coast of Cornwall, England, before nightfall.

By early afternoon, they were about fifty miles offshore and halfway between France and England. As he had been all morning, Captain Doucet was scanning the horizon for ships, and they were constantly looking for anything coming their way. Putting his binoculars in the bulkhead slot next to the steering wheel, he decided it was all clear and gunned the engine, leaving France and the German Occupation behind them. They headed at top speed toward the Southwest coast of England. The plan was to drop anchor in a cove, put the rowboat in the water, and row ashore. The timing had to be right; they needed an incoming tide to help them make landfall.

All was good until the tired diesel engine decided to give up. The captain tried to start it but ran the starter batteries down. They were now drifting. The three men untied the lines securing the rowboat and hauled it over the stern into the water.

The captain growled, "Everyone put life jackets on." He secured the rowboat to a cleat until they could all get aboard. Then, looking at the two women, "OK, you two first." They climbed over the side into the boat. Then, to the men, "Pass down the bags. I'll get water from the galley." He went below, grabbed a gallon of fresh water in a glass bottle with string knotted around the outside, and tossed it up through the companionway into the hands of one of the men. Then he pulled an ax from its strap next to the galley and made holes in the bottom of the boat.

When he climbed back up the companionway steps, the water was nearly up to his knees. The boat was sinking, and its days of fishing and smuggling were over.

The two men got into the rowboat, and the captain followed them. "Look." he pointed to the horizon where they could see a ship's funnel, unsure it was heading in their direction. "My guess is maybe seven or eight miles and about thirty minutes away." The captain growled again.

The two men and the two women each took an oar,

sitting side by side in their rowing station. "Row for your lives," the captain shouted as the little boat bobbed up and down in the rolling sea. As they rowed away, they watched the fishing boat slowly and gracefully disappear below the waves and out of sight of anyone, German, French, or British. Eventually, they were within a few miles of their destination.

A small rowboat approaching a rocky shore under darkness is hard to see among the waves. While it can be dangerous, it is not impossible to navigate. If the British had intercepted them now, it would have been OK for the captain and two passengers. For Bette Carron and Gerhard Moller, AKA Claire and Francois Leblanc, there would be problems.

They saw dark cliffs looming ahead about two miles from the coast. The captain saw a light flash, and he looked at his watch. His 'crew' continued rowing but now getting tired, their bodies hurting. They had blisters on their hands, were wet and hungry, and fatigue was setting in.

Then, after five minutes, another flash of light. He looked at his watch again. "There, that direction." He pointed forward and slightly left from where they were. They rowed hard despite their aching muscles. After five more minutes, another flash of light confirmed the direction and destination. "That's the signal," pointing with an outstretched arm toward the light. "One flash every five minutes for the first fifteen minutes of each hour."

"There," said the captain, "head towards those cliffs into that cove." The wind had picked up a little, blowing onshore, and the incoming tide helped them into the cove.

A voice barely audible over the breaking waves called to them. "Here, throw me a line."Captain Doucette threw the line toward the hardly visible dark shape of someone on land ahead of them. With ropes in their hands, the captain and one of the men quickly jumped out of the boat as it began to wash up on the pebble beach. More voices from people unseen were heard over the sounds of water on the stony beach.

"Here, let me help you with that. Get close."

Then another voice urged the weary crew,

"Quick, get out now."

Hands grabbed each of the women and helped them ashore. "Move to those rocks over there, quickly, hurry up."

Albeit wet, tired, hungry, and frightened for their lives, this rag-tag group had arrived but was not safe yet. There were questions needing answers. The captain realized before they left the anchorage the two who were supposed to be Claire and Francois Leblanc were not who they claimed to be.

Uncle David

Portland, Maine. 1974

Caroline had a busy morning ahead of her. Meetings were planned with the Board, bankers, and lawyers. She expected David around lunchtime and would have a light lunch with him in her office. She needed to talk about her decision and would seek David's support. While he was a shareholder, his vote was not required. Caroline had a majority without his vote and wanted him to remain part of her life. It would be better if he agreed. Caroline had a lot of questions for him, and she was determined to get answers that she believed only David could provide.

It was 8:30. She was running late. Caroline looked at the clock on the bedside table as she pulled on a pair of black pants and tucked her white blouse into the waistband. She put pearls around her neck and small diamond studs in her ears. She checked herself in the mirror and, being satisfied, quickly went downstairs.

Backing the Volvo out of the garage, she turned towards the gate and stopped to pick up the mail, which had been in the mailbox since yesterday. She had forgotten it. She stuffed the small pile of bills, a large brown envelope, and some letters into the bag on the passenger seat next to her. She accelerated away from her house, heading to Route 295. It took her fifteen minutes to get to the office. Traffic was light, and she arrived in good time, but it was still late. Pausing to get a cup of coffee from the flask on the table in the corner of the room, she sat in front of the waiting group. "My apologies for keeping you waiting." Without missing a beat, she moved quickly to the first item on the agenda.

The morning progressed with back-to-back meetings, and then it was lunchtime. Sitting in what used to be Henry's office with a half-eaten sandwich and a semi-warm cup of coffee in front of her, Caroline was quietly reading from an open file. David Preston walked through the open door and pointed back behind him, "Jenny said I should come right in." As soon as she heard David's voice, she closed the folder, stood up, and greeted him with a hug.

"How was China?"

"Tiring, don't ask!"

"I have sandwiches and coffee. Hope that's okay?"

"Works for me," David responded.

Caroline poured coffee from the carafe as David sat down in a chair at the table. They talked about David's trip to China, her decision to sell, and what the future could look like once she is free from her responsibilities.

"Will Robert be coming back? Are you two going to fix the problem between you? You know, his drinking?"

She shrugged, "I don't know." She got up, shut the door, returned to her seat, and looked hard at her Godfather.

"There is something else important I want to discuss."

David had been anticipating this conversation. He crossed his legs, sat back in the chair, looked up casually, and said, "What's that?"

"Frank Lee, Clair Lemoine, The Borderline Hotel, and more."

She continued to look straight at him.

As a politician, David Preston was well-practiced at obfuscating and speaking out of both sides of his mouth. He would tell you some, but not all. He would talk as if that was everything and still tell you nothing. But he did not know just how much Caroline knew and was hoping he could maneuver his way around this anticipated difficult discussion.

"Well, Frank Lee was somebody your dad, and we helped many years ago. As you know, we were both part of logistics and transport for the US Army during the war. In

German-occupied France, some French people desperately wanted to escape to safety in America where they could start a new life."

"That's it," Caroline said, "just helping desperate people?" She was leading him a bit. "So, go on. What happened?"

"Look, we did some things. There was a raging war. We may have slightly stepped over the line. Some things would probably be considered illegal, but back then, you never knew if today would be your last, and you took chances you otherwise would avoid."

Caroline said, "Yes, I can only begin to imagine how that would be." Her sarcasm was apparent, but David was trying to remain casual.

David said, "We did nothing that others were not doing. We helped some people, that's all!"

"While helping yourself, I assume?"

David shifted in his seat. "Well, yes, that's true. It is also true that the money we earned enabled Henry to get going in the trucking business...."

"And Claire Lemoine?"

"Yes, Claire." He paused, his mind racing. "She was once your Dad's friend, and after your mother died, she just reappeared. He had planned to tell you when the time was right but never did, and I think he felt it was a bit of a betrayal of Delores."

Caroline said, "That doesn't make sense to me. It has been years since Mom Died."

David replied, "I know. I encouraged him to tell you, but he insisted he'd tell you when the time was right. Whatever was meant by that, I have no idea. It was while he was in St John, but this was a decade ago. Anyway, they became lovers again. They knew each other during the war in England. But that was before your dad met your mom, and then he bought that Hotel for her. Listen, I am sorry you had to hear that. There was nothing wrong with their relationship." And then, with a shrug, "It's not as if we are living in Victorian times…."

"OK, I get it," Caroline said as she leaned forward with her elbows on the edge of the conference table. "But tell me, and Uncle David, please don't lie to me. I think I know more than you think I know. A lot has happened while you have been away." She told him about Frank Lee's visit, the call to the Hotel Borderline, and how Em was on the other end of the line, listening and calling the police. She told him what Frank Lee had said about her dad getting him on a ship to South America or somewhere else where he would not be found."

David, buying time to think, sipped coffee and picked up a sandwich. The room was cold and silent.

Watching her godfather closely, Caroline added, "The Police have Frank Lee in custody. They picked him up at the toll booth after he left the house."

Again, the room was silent.

David gave a slight shrug of his shoulders.

"David, you don't seem that surprised or concerned?"

He pursed his lips and tilted his head slightly. "No, err, yes. So?"

Caroline's face turned hard. She took a deep breath and went right for what she did not know. She stood up, went to David, and grabbed his arm. Her head bent down, looking him in the face. "So! So? So, the police have told me he, Frank Lee, was a war criminal. A Nazi called Gerhardt Moller. Frank Lee is not his name!" And with the most accusatory tone she could muster, "But you know that, right?"

He pulled his arm away from Caroline's grip and stood up.

She stood up in front of him, blocking his exit. "Don't you dare leave! Frank Lee or Gerhadt Moller, whoever he is, will most likely be sent back to Germany for trial. And now you could be arrested! Do you know that? And for what? Your life, everything in ruins."

She had allowed herself to get mad as hell.

He pulled his arm away. Caroline stood back.

"Listen, if you are too angry to discuss this now. We can talk another time."

She sat down and looked up at David. "Please don't go, stay. Tell me, David, what went on back then in England. Tell me you were not helping Nazis escape. Tell me it was helping persecuted people escape from the Nazis." Caroline was much calmer, and David sat down as she continued. "You and Dad have been hiding something for years, and it looks like the police will find out. They will turn over those stones you would rather not turn."

David sat down again and was stuck searching for the correct answer. There was silence. Then, seeing the only path available, he said, "I know how bad this looks. Your dad and I have lived with this all our lives. We have tried to do things to, well, to compensate, I guess. I will tell you what happened and what Frank Lee and Claire Lemoine know that the police will find out. My life as a Senator will probably be over."

"Caroline said, "Is it that bad?"

He sat thinking, drowning in the silence as he

struggled with where to begin.

"Caroline, it is worse. Nobody ever wanted to hurt you or keep secrets from you, and it is just that when things are in the past, sometimes it is best left that way. When we are young, we make decisions and, looking back on them, wish we had chosen a different course."

"I understand that all too well," she said.

There was some relief in David's voice. A weight he had been carrying for years was about to be lifted. "Your dad and I worked with a French fisherman. His name was Doucette, and we created an escape from Paris to the small island of Ushant. The island is famous for its maritime past and for being a fishing community. It's a key landmark in the Channel approaches. There is a group of islands off the Northwest of France near Le Quanqet, a small coastal town."

Caroline nodded, "Okay, so what happened?"

"Well, it was dangerous for people to get there. The journey of about four hundred miles from Paris could take a week, depending on the roads, troop movements, roadblocks, and bombings by British and American planes. Travelers on this dangerous journey depended on the French underground to help with food, clothing, papers, and safe houses. They were mostly Jews trying to save their lives before being rounded up for transportation to Concentration camps."

Caroline said, "So you were helping people?"

David looked at her with a tear in his eye. "It is true and something we would have been able to talk about, but" he paused and breathed, "Caroline, I am not going to lie to you. Honestly, we were also helping ourselves and did something we, your dad and me, have regretted ever since."

For the next hour, David explained how his life was entwined with Henry's because of what happened in Cornwall years earlier. He talked about how Henry started the company using the money they earned from smuggling people and diamonds from Europe to the U.S.

"Your dad was responsible for transport, and I was responsible for all contacts with the people we needed to make it work. The other two were Reggie and Florence. That's all we knew them as. They would provide a safe house and allow people to rest until they could get the transport your dad organized. It was always something different, depending on what he could wrangle and who he could bribe. The people on the last trip were to be transported to Plymouth first and then to America."

"And?" Caroline asked.

David, who had previously considered several possible explanations, concluded there was no point hiding the truth since the police had Frank Lee.

"Well, there was this time in Cornwall. A small cove somewhere on the coast, Near Penzance."

Caroline got up, went to the bookshelf, and got an Atlas. David joined her, and they bent over to look at a map of England. David ran his fingers across the page.

"There, that was it!" He pointed.

"Really? She shook her head, closed the Atlas, and put it to one side on the table. They both sat down.

"Anyway," David Continued. "The cove was not far from where we had arranged for them to stay for the night. Then there was a problem, one we had never anticipated."

Kill Them Now

Cornwall 1942

They all got ashore safely, wet, tired, hungry, and frightened. The four passengers sat on the ground and were given hot tea from a thermos flask, sandwiches, and blankets.

Captain Doucette held his hand out to Henry Stern as he joined David Preston, Reggie, and Florence Hall. They were to one side of the huddled passengers about 25 feet away. He said, "Sorry, Henry, this is our last trip. I had to sink the boat because we had engine troubles," he added desperately," I didn't know what else to do. So now here I am, and I need to get on that transport. I think it's time for me to follow some of those other poor souls we have helped and get myself to America or anywhere that is not Europe."

"Too bad about the boat; we can arrange papers and transport for you. It's probably time, and we have had a good run." Henry said.

"There is more." Captain Doucette continued. "Those two," pointing to the huddled group, "those two on

266

the right, the man and woman there, are not who they are supposed to be. I think he is German. His accent is not right, and they paid twice the rate without question. And here," pointing to Clair Leblanc, "She is French, but I don't think she is who she says she is. They had the right pass, but that is all. I asked a few questions because, if they were spies, I was in big trouble anyway.

I expected a patrol vessel as we let the mooring go and left the harbor, but it didn't happen. We got away." He looked out across the water, his head lifted slightly, and pointed with his nose toward France."

Reggie said, "We better find out more before we go further." Looking at David, "What do you think?"

David started to answer, but Captain Doucette interrupted. "But here is another thing. The deal agreed with the LeBlancs was for $2500 each." He opened the small canvas bag he had been holding since jumping from the rowboat.

They whispered while the small group sitting on the ground, out of hearing range, just watched.

David held a flashlight into the bag, "So? It looks right to me!" "Well, count it. It's ten thousand." Captain Doucette said and followed up with a question. "So why would they do that? They were to have paid $2500 each, the same as I got from the other two." Looking at the small group, "Something's wrong with those two. I trust my instincts, Henry. We may have been set up."

Henry quickly responded, "But, as you said, you got here without any trouble, so what's the problem?"

"I guess none, apart from the boat breaking down and having to sink it!" Captain Doucette Said.

David then asked, "Did you ask who their contact was?" Captain Doucette replied, "I did. They mumbled and said they never knew his name. At that point, I realized this could be a trap."

Florence, who had been listening, said, "I think we are okay, but I think we should find out more before we do anything."

David agreed, "Let's talk to them and see what we can find out."

Captain Doucette continued. "The other two are from Paris. I'm sure they are good." Then, looking at Henry, "Take my word for it." Then, looking at the pair who called themselves Clair and Francois Leblanc, "They are not the LeBlancs."

"If those two are spies, Nazis" David took a gun from his belt and strode back to the small, huddled group sitting on the ground.

"Who are you?'

Grabbing the man who called himself Francois Leblanc, pulled him to his feet, and holding him from behind, he put the gun to his temple. "Tell me now, or I am blowing your fucking brains out, and then it will not matter anyway."

The woman, Clair Leblanc, protested. Henry had followed David to the group and pulled her away a couple of feet. With his face close to hers, "You stay where you are, don't move, and don't say another word."

He looked at the other two passengers. "And you two, stay where you are. If you move as much as an inch, you will not get off this beach. You all die here, understand?" Both nodded and pulled the blanket closer around themselves.

They remained where they were, not saying a word. They sat close together on the ground, motionless, still wet, and cold.

David turned to the man calling himself Francois Leblanc and, with the gun in the man's face, said, "Well? Who are you? You are not the LeBlancs!"

Meanwhile, Florence and Reggie had moved closer, and all nine people were within a few feet of each other.

Francois Leblanc said, "It's true we are not them.

The Leblancs' name was on a list, and they were caught in a sweep." He looked at David and said, "By now, they are on a train to Drancy in the Northeast of Paris." Trying to sound genuine, he added, "It's a holding camp. Sadly, from there, with many other Jews, they will undoubtedly be worked to death if they are lucky. There is not much hope for them anyway, not much hope for any of us." He played forlorn, hoping it would help if he showed some regret.

He reached into his pocket, and David hit him across the mouth with his gun, "I said you don't fucking move."

Francois Leblanc fell back, a small stream of blood on his cheek. "How did you find out about the transport?" David hit him with the gun again.

"No, wait!" the woman who claimed to be Clair Leblanc got up, "We have more. We can pay more! Show them, do it," she said to her partner.

Francois Leblanc looked at David, who was standing over him and asked for permission. David nodded. The man reached into his pocket and pulled out a white folded piece of paper. Opening, he held it out in front of him.

"See, we have a few diamonds, and it's just enough to help a man make a fresh start. It's all we have." He offered the folded paper to David; he took it and asked,

"How did you get these? Tell me the truth; don't lie.

270

I will know if you are."

Francois did not tell them what happened in Paris. He lied, saying, "I was on a detail that had to go and check homes after people were arrested."

To David, the story sounded weak and did not ring true. Pushing the gun into Francois's ear hard enough to hurt, he said, "You stay there, all of you, don't move.

David, Henry, Captain Doucette, Reggie, and Florence moved away. Standing in a half circle but watching the four passengers, they argued about what to do with the German and his partner. Reggie was adamant.

"She is probably a Nazi as well. They are both lying. No fucking way are we having that scum in our house, not for any amount of money. I'm going to shoot the fucker,"

He pulled a gun from his jacket pocket and was about to approach François Leblanc, but Henry grabbed him. There was a brief struggle as Henry tried to get the weapon from Reggie, but it went off, piercing his heart, and Reggie fell to the ground. Henry stood back, frozen, his eyes wide.

Shocked, Florence rushed over and fell on her now-dead husband. She grabbed the gun and pointed it at Henry; David saw what was happening and, without thinking, shot Florence. With a bullet in her brain, she died before hitting the ground.

The other two passengers panicked, and each pulled out a gun and pointed it at Francois and Clair LeBlanc. Each fired a shot; one missed, and the other grazed Francois' hand. David panicked and shot the two legitimate passengers, who died instantly. It was an action David and Henry would regret for the rest of their lives. It all happened so quickly that it was impossible to stop.

Captain Doucette moved and stood in front of David and pleaded with his hands in the air. "No more, stop, David!" They came to their senses. Francois Leblanc was bleeding, blood coming from his hand and face. Clair Leblanc was in shock, now paralyzed, standing with her back against a rock. At her feet were four dead bodies lying on the ground in little pools of their blood. Reggie and Florence Hall, plus the two other passengers, had become just four more war victims.

Henry and David fell to their knees, shocked at the speed of what had happened. They soon recovered, decided what to do, and then, in silence, they removed all the personal belongings from the four bodies. They found more American Dollars sewn into the coats of one person, twenty thousand dollars of untraceable bearer bonds, and in a bag two more guns, a switchblade. Four bodies were placed in the rowboat and pushed out to sea.

As the little boat drifted into the darkness, five people, Captain Doucette, Bette Carron, Gerhard Moller (The two imposters), David Preston, and Henry Stern, climbed the 50-foot path to the road. They got in a van parked off the side of the road, and Henry drove up a hill and turned right onto a farm road to the house on the right that would be their refuge for the next twenty-four hours.

Over the next couple of days, the tide came in and then out eight times. The rowboat was pounded on the rocks, broke up, and sank. Four bodies were eventually found within fifty yards of each other on a stony beach, with waves rolling the bodies back and forth.

There was a lot of discussion about Florence and Reggie Hall and the unknown identities of the other two bodies. There was a lot of speculation and theories about what had happened. That is until a few days later when the news of the American invasion to liberate Paris came and pushed reporting about the dead bodies away from the front page, eventually forgotten by most people.

Truth Be Told

Portland 1974

Caroline sat silently, processing everything she had just learned about her dad and godfather and their dark history. David, it seemed to Caroline, had suddenly grown old as he struggled to unburden himself and lift the weight of the past from his shoulders. He took a tissue from the box on the table, wiping tears from his cheek. He said, "There, now you know… happy now?"

Caroline did not move or say a word. David glared at Caroline, and said, "You could not let it go, could you? I should never have come here today, and I shan't, ever again." He got up and got ready to leave.

Caroline was stuck, paralyzed, and stunned into silence as she processed what she had just heard. It was as if a building had fallen on top of her, and she was pinned down in the rubble, unable to move or speak. Her mouth felt like it was full of fallen concrete dust. She was still staring at the desk when David, now standing at the door and about to leave, turned and said, "I'm sorry, so sorry. None of it should

ever have happened. But it did. Your dad and me, well…"
He shrugged, turned, walked out, and quietly closed the door
behind him.

Caroline turned her head to the closed door, staring
as her godfather and part of her family walked out of her life
forever. She would never see him again.

A few minutes passed before she got up and took
another look at the atlas. She traced her finger back to what
David had indicated earlier—Mousehole near Penzance,
Cornwall, England. Still processing what she had learned,
she picked up the phone and punched the button on the
phone. Jenny McCarthy answered.

"Jen, I need to cancel with the lawyers. I can't do any more
today, and I'm going home."

Throughout the rest of the day, Caroline was in a stupor.
She wandered around her house, made coffee, let it get cold, made
a sandwich, and left it in the kitchen. Sitting on her bed, looking at
a family photo album, then dropping the album to the floor, curled
up on the bed, and sobbed. Time passed, maybe ten or fifteen
minutes, and then, regaining control of her emotions, she picked up
the phone to call Em. Instead, she made numerous calls to the hotel
in Portland, where Robert had a suite, and left a message with the
hotel.

'Robert, I hope you had a good trip. Call me.

I want to catch up and talk before the kids return tomorrow afternoon.' She then took two sleeping pills and went to sleep.

* * *

Robert's plane touched down in Boston in the early evening. He collected his car from the long-term car park. Two hours later, he checked into the hotel in Portland. A message from Caroline was waiting for him at the front desk. It was late, and he was tired from jet lag but pleased to have a message from Caroline. He threw his suitcase and shoulder bag on the bed and, looking at his watch, decided it was not too late to call.

Caroline was restless; the pills were no longer working, and she could not sleep. She lay on her back in the darkness, and in her mind, she played many different scenarios: the events David described, what she would say to Robert, and how she would tell her children. Her mind was churning. The bedside phone rang. She sat up and shook her head as she tried to 'get her brain in gear.'

"Hi Caroline, I'm back and got your message. Everything OK?"

"Robert, hi," she said, stumbling for words. Thanks for calling. I'm glad you're back. Yes, all is good," she lied. I just wanted to talk and see how the trip went. Just catch up, you know, before the kids get back."

"That would be nice. Caroline, I found out things in Cornwall, things about what happened to me when I was a child. I don't know where to start. It's a bit overwhelming, and it's just," and searching for the words. "But anyway, I am feeling weary, jet lag and that. How about breakfast in the morning?"

"Well, okay." She paused and briefly considered asking him to come immediately but quickly thought better of it. "Ah, err, yes, that sounds good. See you around eight at home?"

"Sure, look forward to it." Robert put the phone down, thinking, 'Home, that sounds good. Maybe there is hope.' He slept soundly.

The following morning, Robert pulled into the driveway and parked his car in front of the garage. The front door was not locked, and he walked in and called, "Hi Caroline, hope the coffee is hot!" Walking into the kitchen, he found Caroline sitting on the highchair at the kitchen island.

"I missed American coffee in England."

She got up, turned, put her hand on his shoulder, and kissed him on the cheek. It was the first time they had been together since she had told him there would be no 'us' and she could not live under the same roof as him.

A tray with fresh croissants, some fruit, and yogurt was on the counter in front of them. Robert poured himself coffee from the carafe. Caroline picked up the tray and walked away. "Let's go to the den." She said.

They sat corner to corner—Caroline on the couch and Robert on one of the easy chairs.

"So, what's been happening at Stern."

Caroline rolled her eyes, "It has been difficult, but I think we are over the hump."

They discussed her decision to sell and that Frank Lee was now in custody. Keeping it vague, "Apparently, his real name is Gerhard Moller – he may be a war criminal."

"What, like a Nazi?"

"I guess so." She did not mention meeting him at Henry's house.

"I had a weird conversation with Uncle David yesterday."

"Weird, in what way?"

"Well, that thing with Frank Lee, it seems Uncle David knew the guy from back in the war." Shifting uncomfortably on the couch, "My dad, too. You remember the note that caused me to go to Boston to look for him."

"What, what are you talking about? How could they

be involved with war criminals? I don't believe it. How could that be?"

"Not sure yet. That's all I can tell you just now." It was all she could do to grasp what she had begun to understand. First, she needed to be sure. "The police are investigating. We will know more soon. I guess. We can call David later for an update. As far as I know, he will speak to them today."

"Well, at least you didn't rush to Canada looking for some woman! I am glad about that."

"Yes, she is genuine and was my dad's lover."

Robert opened his eyes wide. "If that is all there is to it, that is not our business. Your dad was alone for long enough, so who could blame him?

Caroline agreed, moving the conversation on, "Anyway, I want to hear more about your trip.

Robert felt happy, and with Caroline being so friendly to him, his hopes of getting back together were rising. "I am not sure where to start." His voice was steady, the dark shadows around his eyes gone. He looked relaxed, even if a bit jet-lagged from the journey. It seemed to Caroline that he was more like Robert, whom she knew and fell in love with a lifetime ago.

"Okay, you know some of what I found out at the

therapy sessions in rehab." Caroline nodded. "Well, I also researched in their library, making phone calls, but you know that, sorry. So anyway, I went to a small town down on the coast, near Penzance. It turned out that my parents lived not far from there. I met my childhood friend, Walter Hammet, and my old schoolteacher. She now runs the local Post Office. I found the house where I grew up, even the carving I made in the corner of a shed when I lived there. The woman who lives there now invited me in." Caroline was nodding, encouraging him to continue without interruption. "She was so friendly and told me about other people in the village I could talk to."

Caroline's heart was pounding. She listened but did not understand. Her mind wandered to the questions she desperately wanted to ask.

"Anyway, I found their graves, Mom and Dad, in a little church cemetery not far from where I grew up. And this is shocking to me; I have not come to terms with it yet. My parents' bodies were found floating in the ocean."

"Are you sure, Robert?" She was afraid of the answer but was becoming more certain she was correct about her conclusions, so she had to check the details.

"When I think about it, I get feelings I have ignored, pushed away, it seems forever. At rehab, they told me to let go and experience anger, love, or confusion. They encouraged me to go with the flow, but I am getting away from myself."

"Yes." Caroline agreed, "What else?"

"I spoke to a local Police inspector who was there at the time. He remembered all the speculation and gossip. Back then, he was a constable, you know, low rank. He told me they were killed. Dad was shot in the heart and Mom in the head." He choked up, tears in his eyes, caught in emotional memory. "I am coming to terms with it, but it's been a long journey. I didn't expect that, but finding out about it now seems to change my view of the world. The flight home gave me time to think about putting my life, you know, put it in perspective. I don't understand how this happened, what led to their murder, and how I ended up unconscious and in the hospital. Did somebody try to kill me?

Caroline interrupted, "How could you possibly expect that? It's terrible."

"Yes, and it makes me mad when I think about it. Why would Uncle William not tell me? He must have known. Perhaps he thought he was protecting me somehow? Why did he bring me to America and never tell me what he knew?"

Caroline responded, "Maybe he was going to, but then there was that hit and run."

"Yes, well, it's all history now. I understand much more and can put it all in the past. I have my notebook with my drawings in the car and films to develop. I want to return with you and the kids soon." She ignored the invitation.

"I'll get my notepad from the car. I have some sketches to show you." He put his hands on the arms of the chair and was about to get up but sat back down, "But first, I want to hear more about this thing with Uncle David. It sounds as if it could be serious?"

"Robert, I found out that Dad and David did some bad stuff when they were younger." She was dancing around what she wanted to say. "This is going to sound, well, I can't believe this." She hesitated.

"What are you trying to tell me, Caroline?"

She took a deep breath and said, "They were smuggling people from France to America during the war."

She studied Robert, looking for a reaction.

Robert blinked. "What?"

"Jews mostly, from Paris, and they set up an escape route and helped those they could. They were mostly people the Nazis wanted out of the way, destined to be sent to work and concentration camps."

Robert said, "That doesn't seem so bad. It sounds like they could be heroes?"

"I wish that were the case, but that is not the whole story. Dad and David were in Army Transport Services, logistics. They had a private enterprise, helping desperate people cross the English Channel to England and Cornwall. It was the nearest place to cross, where they had a chance not to be caught."

"That is what David told you? It doesn't sound like a bad thing." He shook his head and continued, "Cornwall, they got them to Cornwall?" He asked, but it was more of a statement. "That is such a weird coincidence. Now I know we were meant for each other for sure!" Robert continued, "I was not going to mention this just yet, but in Cornwall, I sat overlooking the bay where my parents died. Having learned what happened and being back there, probably in the same spot, my memories came back. I remember being there as a kid. It was night, and I had left my bed and went outside to look for them. I wandered up to a hill overlooking the ocean and looked down into the little cove with a stony beach. As a child, I remember seeing my parents killed. I am guessing it was Germans, and my mom and dad stumbled upon German spies. I don't think there can be any other explanation."

Caroline sat, immobilized—her tummy in a tight knot.

"I think I saw them killed. At least, it seems that way." Robert described what he had seen as a child and choked more tears away. Memories buried deep in his mind were now front and center. "The cove, it was next to the village of Mousehole."

Caroline now looked as if she had seen a ghost. The blood drained from her face. She looked down, very slightly shaking her head, almost imperceptibly, and said, more to herself than Robert, "No."

Not knowing what to make of her look, Robert said, "I know, it's a strange name, but you can find it on the map.

"I have," she said very quietly. "What do you remember about what happened?"

Robert described what happened before he fell and passed out. He looked over at Caroline and suddenly noticed her despair. "What's wrong? Why are you shaking?".

Caroline stood up. "I am going to be sick!".

Robert had described the same scene from a different perspective- than David had described yesterday in her office, but there was no doubt in her mind that it was the same.

Caroline yelled out, "NO, NO!" She sobbed

uncontrollably. She was struck with grief, an overwhelming fear as if swept from a ship, and nobody saw her fall. She was lost to all and drowning in a dark and foreboding sea.

She stood up, saying, "You must leave. You can't be here!"

Robert remained seated. "No, I am not going anywhere. Talk to me. What is going on?" He encouraged her to sit back down and stayed beside her, trying to console her. He was hesitant to touch her, but he put his hand on her arm, and she allowed it.

"Robert, I can't.' I just can't. It's too much, your parents, Reggie, and Florence." And between sobs, "God, please tell me I am wrong."

"About what, for Christ's sake?" He was now getting impatient with Caroline.

She managed to get control of herself and turned slightly towards him, her head down and looking half at him through her tears. "Robert," she said as she cried, between breaths, "Robert...." The words just would not come out. "Robert, please, please forgive me. Forgive me," she cried. "Oh god, Robert, please tell me I am wrong. Tell me you were not there."

Robert felt himself getting impatient and demanded, "Not where?

"In Cornwall, in that village, Mousehole. That is not where you were, right? Tell me you haven't been there, not there!"

"What do you mean? I was just there, I told you." Now, he was getting agitated. "Why, what have you done? Tell me."

Caroline just blurted it out, "Not me, I think. I think"

She paused again as she struggled to find the words she needed. "I think my father killed your parents."

He pulled back from her. "What are you talking about?"

Through her tears and convulsing sobs, she managed to describe the rest of what David had told her and, she imagined, what it was that Robert probably had seen as a child. Robert and Caroline compared more of what they each had found out. They put it all together, and, between what Caroline had heard from David and what Robert had found out in rehab and on his trip to Cornwall, they came to the only conclusion they could. They sat in silence, all the air gone from the room.

Robert finally spoke, calm at first, but a volcano was building inside of him that was about to erupt. "All my life, I have felt as if I have been in mid-sentence, like when a word would not come to mind. I have lived with a constant feeling of dread. I have been hanging on an edge, reaching out for safety just beyond my grasp."

Now, he was getting hot. His anger was beginning to find an expression. "Throughout my life, I have felt like I had fallen into an abyss. I have always felt lost."

He paused and put his head in his hands. He looked up, out across the room and away from Caroline. Then, turning towards her and raising his voice," It's as if I have been climbing a cliff to see what lies beyond and never quite being able to get there." Confusion and anger washed over him. "I have never felt satisfied. I've always felt it deep down inside, a longing for something unexplained."

She sat there quietly sobbing, crying for her world, which had been slowly unraveling since Henry disappeared and was found dead. She was numb, her misplaced guilt and helplessness pressing on her, tearing her between love and hate. Love for her dad and uncle and hating them because of what they had done. They had ruined so many lives. It felt as if some unforeseen hand was taking revenge, punishing the children for the parent's sins. She turned to Robert and was about to tell him how she loved him, but he exploded.

He stood up, angry, his face showing deep lines, and yelled. "What, what…all these years? Murderers, both! With all their wealth and fancy careers, they are nothing but murderers." Not knowing what to do with the emotions overtaking him, he burst out, "And you have been slowly murdering me with all your demands and instructions, your father's daughter."

He swept his hands across the table and sent the coffee, croissant, sugar, milk, cups, and plates flying across the room. His head shaking, body trembling, he went to the door.

"Stay away from me, don't call or talk to me." He rushed out the door, got in his car, and headed for Portland.

Caroline looked after him, begging him to stop and stay with her. But he was gone. She turned back into the den, got down on her hands and knees, and began to pick up the broken crockery and became overcome with grief. She collapsed and lay on the floor, crying her heart out, curling up like a newborn.

* * *

Robert was now driving on Route 95. He pushed his foot on the gas and accelerated. He was doing close to 100 as he looked down at the speedometer; a voice in his head said, "Robert, wake up…wake up!" He immediately took his foot off the gas, and the car slowed. He was out of his mind, and as if in a dream, he drove to the offices of Stern Trucking and Shipping, parked the car, and went to his office.

Opening the door, he went straight to the closet where, under a box of old files, he retrieved an unopened bottle of vodka and took it and a glass to his desk. He sat looking at his half-finished drawing for the new offices he had been working on with the question in red ink scrawled across it: Where is Henry?

Robert stood up and threw everything on his desk across the floor. He opened his file drawer, grabbed all the files, and scattered them. He then turned furniture over, tore up more drawings, pulled everything off the walls, and threw them across the room. He collapsed and sat panting on the floor. Perspiration ran down his forehead, getting into his eyes and stinging. He got up on his knees as if about to pray, picked up the unopened bottle of vodka, clinched it with both hands, and pressed it to his forehead.

* * *

Caroline got up and went to the phone on the little table next to the armchair. She called Em, and before Em could say anything, she blurted out, "He's gone, Em. I don't know where he's gone."

And between breaths, "Or what he will do." She was trying to get her breath.

"Who, Caroline? What are you talking about? What's wrong?"

"Robert, I told him everything Em. Henry and David killed his Mom and Dad, and now Robert is gone."

"Caroline, what in the name of Christ are you talking about?

Who killed who?" Em was raising her voice in confusion.

"I can't explain now; it's too much. It's bad, really bad." Caroline was now looking out the window, staring towards the front gate, hoping to see Robert's car return to the driveway.

Em said, "I have no idea what you have done, but…"

"No, not me, not me, Em. It was Dad, David, and that creep Frank Lee, back in the war," Caroline very briefly and quickly tried to explain.

Em was listening. "Okay, right now, it's Robert. We have to be concerned about"?

"Yes, I don't know where he is. After I told him, he left and drove out through the gate like a mad person."

Just responding to her friend's distress, Emily interrupted Caroline, "Maybe he has gone to the hotel. Put the phone back on the hook, and I will call. OK, hold on."

Caroline waited. It seemed like forever. After a couple of minutes, the phone rang. She picked it up and did not allow Em to speak,

"Well, is he there?"

"No, but I left a message. I don't know what's happening, but maybe he went to his office? Hold on, I will call. Hang up. I will be a minute."

Caroline sat on the couch, rocking, with the phone on her lap and her arms around her knees. A minute later, it rang, and Caroline grabbed at it.

Em said, "The line was busy, but I spoke to Jenny, and she said his car was there."

"Okay, can you go there, Em? You can be there in ten minutes, which will take me twenty minutes. You go. I will meet you there?"

Em responded, not understanding what Caroline was trying to tell her. "Hold on a minute.

If you've fought, I don't think I should get in between you and Robert."

"Em, it's more than a fight! It's the reason for Robert not knowing about his childhood, and now he knows everything, every horrid detail." Caroline took a deep breath. "Please, Em, I just need to know he is okay and to talk to him."

"All right, but drive slowly. I don't want any accidents. I will be there when you arrive."

* * *

Em arrived at Robert's office, but he was gone. The

place was a mess, and she began picking things up but decided to leave things as they were and left the building to wait for Caroline, who arrived ten minutes later.

Em looked at her and said, "My God, you look awful." She reached out and put her hand on Caroline's shoulder. "He was here. The place is a wreck; everything is upside down, thrown all over the floor.

Caroline interrupted, "He has gone to Dad's house. I know it!

* * *

Robert turned off Rte. 95 and drove through the outskirts of Portland, over Casco Bay bridge, telling himself to calm down. But a fire was burning inside him, and the still unopened bottle of vodka was on the seat beside him.

He turned past the stone wall through the gate and stopped a few yards from the house. He picked up the bottle of vodka from the passenger seat and walked up the four stone steps to the house. Standing in the entryway, he raised his hands to a ledge above the door and got the spare key. He went in, and as he walked past the side table, he grabbed it and pushed it across the floor. The table turned over, and the vase crashed to pieces. He went up the stairs to Henry's bedroom and his dressing room. He grabbed some of his clothes—suits, shirts, and ties— and threw them in a pile on the floor at the end of the bed. He opened drawers and threw things across the floor but could not find what he wanted. Robert was in another world, panting and sweating, not knowing what he was doing.

The rug got itself curled up, and he noticed the safe, "What is this, you sneaky shithead?" he said aloud. He saw the previously hidden safe and tried to open it. Pulling the handle again, Robert shouted for the world to hear. "Fuck you, Henry, fuck you, David," Picking up the bottle of vodka he had dropped on the floor, he took as many clothes as he could from the pile and headed downstairs with his arms wrapped around them, still holding the bottle of vodka with his fingers locked around it. It was awkward for him to hold onto everything, and he stumbled down the stairs, leaving a trail of clothes behind him.

He went into the Lion's Den, threw what clothes he still had in his hands on the floor, and pulled books from the shelf, tearing them apart as he added them to the pile. He opened a file cabinet, tossed all the folders into the pile, and turned the desk over.

Next, he went to the kitchen and pulled out one drawer after the other, allowing their contents to fall on the floor. He found the matches he had been looking for and returned to Henry's study.

He then sat in Henry's chair, unscrewed the cap from the bottle of vodka, and poured it on the stack of books and clothes. Striking a match and throwing the rest on the pile, he set fire to it and watched as the flames engulfed the remains of Henry's secrets.

He said aloud, "Burn in Hell, Henry."

* * *

On the drive to Henry's house, Caroline explained to Em what had happened as best she could. She turned the car through the front gate. Robert's car was there, doors open, but there was no immediate sign of him. Both women exited the car and quickly went to the front door. Fire alarms were screeching from inside, and then the urgent whining of fire trucks in the distance. They walked into a rainstorm. Water was dripping from the sprinkler system. Em called out, "Robert, where are you?"

Caroline turned and went into Henry's study and found her husband sitting on the floor crying, legs pulled up to his chest with his arms clasped in front. The fire he had started was smoldering, the walls covered with soot. Robert was drenched, and now Caroline was as well—her red hair in strands on her face, wet and bedraggled.

"Robert," she said as she gently touched his arm. He looked up. "Let's go home, don't do this."

Em came into the room, wide-eyed and soaked.

Caroline looked at her, "The shut-off, it's in the basement." Em turned around and went to deal with it. The 'rainstorm' stopped, and shortly, Em returned to Henry's study, where she joined Caroline at Robert's side. Caroline was sitting next to him, arm around his shoulder.

Em touched Robert's arm and gently said, "Come on, let's go home."

Both women helped Robert get up and walked him towards the front door as three fire trucks, an ambulance, and a police car arrived. It took a while, but soon, everything was secured in the house. The police were sympathetic and told Caroline they had to go to the police station within 48 hours to make a full report.

Em, Caroline, and Robert got into Caroline's car, and Em drove them home. Caroline sat in the back with Robert. All three were a mess. Wrapped in silvery survival blankets given to them by the fire department, they were wet, cold, and miserable.

The storm had passed, and Robert had calmed down. His emotional and cathartic outburst complete, he turned to Caroline. "I never knew my parents, and Henry and David cheated me of my childhood. I wish I had never found out."

Caroline said, "I know, I know." There was silence

for a moment, and then she said, "Maybe we can fix this. At least we can try."

"I don't think I can," said Robert. "Can you? Your dad, the one person in the world you adored, respected, and loved, deceived you all his life. I'm glad he's dead. If he were not, he would be...."

"Robert," Caroline said, "He was not the only one, not the only person I respect and love." She put her arms around him and held him close. "You are my life, my heart, and soul. I love you. We have a family to protect, and we need to see them grow and have their own children. I want us to be grandparents together, and we can make this right."

There was silence.

Loose Ends

Two days later, David Preston, the senator from Maine, was found dead. The autopsy revealed he had been dead for at least 24 hours from an overdose of barbiturates. It was before the FBI interviewed him, and it made front-page news. The story was quickly replaced by the unfolding of President Nixon's Watergate scandal.

None of the characters ever told me how Henry's relationship developed with Claire while she was waiting for transport to America. While she probably did tell him that she had worked with the resistance, It is doubtful she told him the whole truth of what had happened, what she and Gerhard Moller had done in Paris before escaping from the Nazis. However, their past caught up with them, and they were sent back to Germany to face trial. Gerhardt Moller lived to be an old man and died in prison. I could not find out what happened to Bette Caron after she was sent back to Germany. I asked, but none of the characters would tell me.

Captain Doucet was negligent and never correctly checked all passengers for weapons before they got on his boat. If he had, the entire mess would have been avoided.

Caroline never read the mail she stuffed into that oversized bag the day David Preston told her what he knew. If she had, perhaps she would have been better prepared because she would have seen Robert had sent her a postcard from a little village called Mousehole on the rugged coast of Cornwall, England.

Caroline and Em did eventually quit smoking.

A Camp by The Lake

Maine 1990

Summer camps in Maine are generally used for a few months of the year. Usually, they are modest, often rustic, and without running water. They may have a water well and sometimes only an outhouse and an outdoor shower for a bathroom. Typically, they have wood fires that help to extend the season through the fall and then are closed for the winter; pipes drained, outdoor furniture covered and stored.

There is no better place to be in the summer months when kids are on vacation from school. You can swim in a lake, sail a boat, make a campfire, cook S'mores, hike a mountain, or wander in the woods. The camps on Megunticook Lake, about a ten-minute drive from the town of Camden, vary in size and amenities. Everything from a simple shack to a home most of us could only dream of owning but would be happy to rent for a summer vacation.

The Hall family camp had a modest footprint. Still, it had three bathrooms, four bedrooms, a great room, and a three-season porch extending out over the lake's edge. It had a grassy backyard with a barbecue pit; around it, half a dozen Adirondack chairs made of cedar wood, dulling to a light silvery color.

There was a large oak tree, and carefully secured to it was a swing where a young girl was pushed by her dad. Michael Hall was now thirty, and the memory of his Granddad, Henry Stern, had faded into a distant and sad memory. Like the rest of his family, he came to terms with that terrible time back in 1974 when it seemed like the world was ending. Michael was now married with a daughter. Her fourth birthday party was planned for this weekend.

Michael was smiling as he looked across the lawn to see his mom, Caroline, coming out onto the porch, pushing open the screen door and allowing it to slam behind her. She was carrying a jug of iced tea and glasses on a tray. She called Michael, "Cold drinks if you want them?" He acknowledged with a nod and started back up to the house with his daughter, Evelyn, in his arms.

"When is mommy coming?" Little Evy asked.

"Soon, this afternoon," Michael said as he tickled her tummy.

A lot has happened to the world in the past fifteen years. There was talk about the World Wide Web, and Nelson Mandela was released from prison in South Africa. The

Hubble telescope was launched into space, Iraqi forces invaded Kuwait, and Caroline and Michael Hall became grandparents. They had worked through their problems, forgiven each other, and resumed their lives together.

Robert had been in some private reverie watching his eldest son and granddaughter play in the afternoon sun. When the screen door slammed, he sat up startled. He quickly removed his feet from the small table before him, and Caroline set the jug of iced tea and glasses down. She poured a glass, handed it to Robert, poured one for herself, and sat beside him on the porch.

Robert took the glass and said, "She reminds me of Melissa at that age, so full of joy."

Caroline smiled, "Yes, she does. By the way, she just called and is meeting Em, and they will drive up together this weekend for the party."

Robert smiled. "I can't believe she's graduating soon. Where did the years go?'

Caroline nodded, furrowed her eyebrows, and almost whispered, "Yes, where did they go?"

"What about Richard?" Asked Robert. "I assume he will be here.

I worry about him sometimes, and I think he is a bit too young to consider marriage."

Caroline looked at Robert, put her hand on his knee, and smiled at him with her head to one side, she said,

"They will be fine."

About the Author

Writing this novel was an experiment to see if I could. It has been a great learning experience. Writing a story was just the beginning. Getting through multiple edits, revisions, corrections, and publishing has been a journey. I hope you enjoy the story.

John Alexander

In my 20s, I ran overland tours to India, Nepal, and North Africa. After returning to the UK, I owned three electronics stores. I sold consumer electronics, components, and services.

Before being captured by my wife and brought to America in 1993, I was a partner of Synectics UK, a consulting firm based in Cambridge, MA. We focused on creative problem-solving, teamwork, and communication skills in corporate decision-making.

I lived in Rockport, Maine, where I owned two seasonal campgrounds, and now find tranquility and inspiration in Portland, Maine.

www.ingramcontent.com/pod-product-compliance
Lightning Source LLC
Chambersburg PA
CBHW071711120626
46550CB00001B/185